VOGUE CHILDREN'S KNITS

Christina Probert

Prentice Hall Press · New York

Acknowledgements

Colour photographs by Mario Testino.

Black and white photographs by Bailey 10; Honeyman 62; Lousada 17; Ogden 30.

Hair by Layla D'Angelo 4, 12, 18, 19, 25, 31, 34, 39, 43, 45, 50, 53, 55; Mitch Barry 8, 15, 16, 21, 22, 28, 33, 37, 40, 47, 48, 52, 57, 59, 64.

Published by Prentice Hall Press
A division of Simon & Schuster, Inc.
Gulf + Western Building
One Gulf + Western Plaza
New York, N.Y. 10023

Originally published by Angell Editions, Newton Abbot, Devon

PRENTICE HALL PRESS is a trademark of Simon & Schuster, Inc.

Library of Congress Cataloging-in-Publication Data

Probert, Christina,
  Vogue children's knits.

  (Vogue knitting library; 6)
  1. Chilren's clothing. 2. Knitting – Patterns.
I. Vogue (New York) II. Title. III. Series.
TT825.P76   1986   746.9'2   86-18710

ISBN 0-13-943028-8

Printed in The Netherlands

10 9 8 7 6 5 4 3 2 1

First Prentice Hall Press Edition

Contents

Yarn Conversion Chart   Inside front cover
Needle Conversion Chart   Inside front cover

PATTERNS
Tucked Woollen Dress 1951   5
Three-colour Norwegian Twin Set 1959   7
Diagonal-stitch Cardigan 1935   10
Lacy-yoked Sweater 1951   12
Two-colour, Zig-zag Cardigan 1961   14
Fisherman's-rib, Round-neck Sweater 1982   17
Flower-pattern Dress 1948   18
Twisted-stitch Slipover 1936   20
Flower-pattern, Fair Isle Sweater 1960   23
Duck-pattern Shirt 1949   24
Twin Set with Cabled Raglans 1954   27
Vest with Garter-stitch Yoke 1936   30
Shoulder-buttoning Nautical Sweater 1955   32
Satin-edged Lacy Shawl 1949   34
Sweater with Circular-ribbed Yoke 1961   36
Chunky, Moss-stitch Jacket 1942   38
Double-breasted Cotton Shirt 1938   41
Russian Blouse 1933   42
Round-neck, Buttoned Playshirt 1948   44
Woven-stitch Knitted Shirt 1955   46
Thick Cotton Sleeveless Pullover 1935   48
Polka-dot Jacket 1950   49
Sweater with Cabled Cross-stitch 1949   51
Raised Pattern Sweater 1960   52
Ridged Stocking Stitch Sweater 1935   54
Square-necked, T-shirt Sweater 1954   56
Rabbit-design Sweater 1954   58
Sleeveless Pullover in Cross-stitch 1937   61
Twinset with Round or V-neckline 1957   62

Addresses of Stockists   Inside back cover

Tucked Woollen Dress

1951

Fine wool and angora dress with tucked skirt and bodice, puffed sleeves, long back button opening and doubled hems

★★★ Suitable for experienced knitters only

MATERIALS

Yarn
Jaeger Luxury Spun 4 ply
5(5:6:6) × 50g. balls

Needles
1 pair 2¾mm.
1 pair 3¼mm.
2 st. holders

Buttons
7

MEASUREMENTS

Chest
46(51:56:61) cm.
18(20:22:24) in.
6 months/1(1/2:2/3:4/5) approx. age

Length
42(46:49:53) cm.
16½(18:19¼:20¾) in.

Sleeve Seam
7(7:9:9) cm.
2¾(2¾:3½:3½) in.

TENSION

28 sts. and 36 rows = 10 cm. (4 in.) square over st. st. on 3¼mm. needles. If your tension square does not correspond to these measurements, adjust the needle size used.

ABBREVIATIONS

k. = knit; p. = purl; st(s). = stitch(es); inc. = increas(ing); dec. = decreas(ing); beg. = begin(ning); rem. = remain(ing); rep. = repeat; alt. = alternate; tog. = together; sl. = slip (transfer one stitch from left needle, knitwise unless otherwise stated, to right hand needle.); cont. = continue; patt. = pattern; foll. = following; folls. = follows; mm. = millimetres; cm. = centimetres; in. = inches; st. st. = stocking st.: one row k., one row p.; g. st. = garter st.: every row k.; incs. = increases; decs. = decreases; m.1 = make 1 st.: pick up horizontal loop lying before next st. and work into the back of it; y.fwd. = yarn forward; t.b.l. = through back of loops.

FRONT

** Cast on 105(121:137:153) sts. with 2¾mm. needles.
Work 12 rows in st. st., beg. with a k. row.
Next row: p.
The last row forms ridge for hemline.
Work a further 13 rows in st. st., beg. with a p. row.
Make hem by k. 1 st. from needle tog. with 1 st. from cast-on edge all along row.
Change to 3¼mm. needles, cont. in st. st.
Work a further 25 rows straight.
Next row: p.
Work a further 9 rows in st. st., beg. with a p. row.
To make 1st tuck: fold work on p. ridge, counting down 9 rows from ridge on wrong side of work and k. 1 st. from needle tog. with 1 st. from 10th row all along row.
Work 23 rows in st. st., beg. with a p. row.
Next row: p.
Work a further 7 rows in st. st., beg. with a p. row.
2nd tuck: fold work on p. ridge as before and k. 1 st. from needle tog. with 1 st. from 8th row all along row.
Work 21 rows in st. st., beg. with a p. row.
Next row: p.
Work 5 rows in st. st., beg. with a p. row.
3rd tuck: work as before by k. 1 st. from needle tog. with 1 st. from 6th row all along row.
Work 19 rows in st. st., beg. with a p. row.
Next row: p.
Work 3 rows in st. st., beg. with a p. row.
4th tuck: k. 1 st. from needle tog. with 1 st. from 4th row all along row.
Beg. with a p. row, cont. straight in st. st. until front measures 23(25:28:30) cm. (9(9¾:11:11¾) in.) at centre, ending with a k. row. **

Shape Skirt
Next row: p.1, * p.2 tog., rep. from * to end. [53(61:69:77) sts.]
Change to 2¾mm. needles.
Work 14 rows in st. st.
Next row: k.4(3:3:2), m.1, * k.5(6:7:8), m.1, rep. from * to last 4(4:3:3) sts., k.4(4:3:3). [63(71:79:87) sts.]

Change to 3¼mm. needles and cont. in st. st. until front measures 33(36:38:41) cm. (13(14:15:16) in.) at centre, ending with a p. row.
Work a further 6 rows straight.
Next row: p.
Work 5 rows in st. st., beg. with a p. row.
Make tuck as for 3rd tuck on skirt.
Next row: p.

Shape Armholes
Cast off 4 sts. at beg. of next 2 rows.
Now dec. 1 st. at each end of every row until 49(53:57:61) sts. rem.
Next row: p.
Work a further 4 rows straight.
Next row: p.
Work 3 rows in st. st., beg. with a p. row.
Make tuck as for 4th tuck on skirt.
Cont. in st. st. until front measures 37(41:44:48) cm. (14½(16:17¼:18¾) in.) at centre, ending with a p. row.

Divide for Neck
Next row: k.12(13:14:15), turn and leave rem. sts. on spare needle.
Cont. on these 12(13:14:15) sts. for first side.
Work 17 rows straight.
Cast off.
With right side facing, sl. centre 25(27:29:31) sts. onto a spare needle.
Rejoin yarn to rem. sts., k. to end.
Complete to correspond with first side.

BACK

Work as for front from ** to **.

Shape Skirt
Next row: p.1, (p.2 tog.) 26(30:34:38) times, turn and leave rem. sts. on a spare needle.
Change to 2¾mm. needles and cont. on these 27(31:35:39) sts. for first side as folls.:
Next row: cast on 2, k. to end. [29(33:37:41) sts.]
Now, k. 5 sts. at centre back edge on every row throughout, work a further 13 rows straight.
Next row: k.7(9:9:9), m.1, * k.5(5:6:7), m.1, rep. from * to last 2(4:4:4) sts., k.2(4:4:4). [34(38:42:46) sts.]
Change to 3¼mm. needles and cont. in st. st. until back matches front to armhole at side edge, ending with a k. row.

5

Shape Armhole

Cast off 4 sts. at beg. of next row.
Now dec. 1 st. at armhole edge on every row until 27(29:31:33) sts. rem.
Work straight until back measures 39(43:46:50) cm. (15¼(16¾:18:19½) in.) at centre, ending with a wrong side row.

Shape Neck

Next row: sl. first 15(16:17:18) sts. onto holder, rejoin yarn to rem. 12(13:14:15) sts. and work straight until back matches front at armhole edge.
Cast off.
Next row: with wrong side facing, rejoin

yarn to rem. 52(60:68:76) sts., cast on 3 sts., k.3, (k.2 tog.) twice, (p.2 tog.) 24(28:32:36) times. [29(33:37:41) sts.]
Change to 2¾mm. needles and complete to match 1st side, reversing all shapings and making 6 buttonholes, 1st to come 1 cm. (½ in.) above beg. of border, 6th 2 cm. (¾ in.) below neck shaping, and rem. spaced evenly between.
Mark position of buttons on left border with pins to ensure even spacing, then work holes to correspond.
Buttonhole row (right side): k. to last 4 sts., k.2 tog., y.fwd., k.2.

SLEEVES

Cast on 38(42:46:50) sts. with 2¾mm. needles.
Work 4 rows in st. st., beg. with a k. row.
Next row: p.
Work a further 5 rows in st. st., beg. with a p. row.
Make hem in next row as for skirt.
Next row: p.1, * m.1, p.1, rep. from * to end. [75(83:91:99) sts.]
Change to 3¼mm. needles.
Cont. in st. st. until sleeve measures 7(7:9:9) cm. (2¾(2¾:3½:3½) in.) at centre, ending with a p. row.

Shape Top

Cast off 4 sts. at beg. of next 2 rows.
Now dec. 1 st. at each end of every row until 39(39:39:39) sts. rem.
Next row: k.1, * k.2 tog., rep. from * to end. [20 sts.]
Cast off.

NECKBORDER

Sew up shoulder seams.
With right side facing and 2¾mm. needles beg. at left side of back opening and k. 15(16:17:18) sts. from holder, pick up and k.8 sts. up left side of back, 16 sts. down left side of front, k.25(27:29:31) sts. from centre, pick up and k.16 sts. up right side of front, 8 sts. down right side of back, then k.15(16:17:18) sts. from holder. [103(107:111:115) sts.]

1st, 3rd and 5th rows: k.5, p. to last 5 sts., k.5.
2nd row: k. 13(14:15:16), k.2 tog. t.b.l., k.2 tog., k.20, k.2 tog. t.b.l., k.2 tog., k.21(23:25:27), k.2 tog. t.b.l., k.2 tog., k.20, k.2 tog. t.b.l., k.2 tog., k.13(14:15:16). [95(99:103:107) sts.]
4th row: k.12(13:14:15), k.2 tog. t.b.l., k.2 tog., k.18, k.2 tog. t.b.l., k.2 tog., k.19(21:23:25), k.2 tog. t.b.l., k.2 tog., k.18, k.2 tog. t.b.l., k.2 tog., k.8(9:10:11), k.2 tog., y.fwd., k.2. [87(91:95:99) sts.]
6th row: k.11(12:13:14), k.2 tog. t.b.l., k.2 tog., k.16, k.2 tog. t.b.l., k.2 tog., k.17(19:21:23), k.2 tog. t.b.l., k.2 tog., k.16, k.2 tog. t.b.l., k.2 tog., k.11(12:13:14). [79(83:87:91) sts.]
Next row: cast off 5 sts., k. to end.
Next row: cast off 5 sts., k.6(7:8:9), inc. in each of next 2 sts., k.16, inc. in each of next 2 sts., k.17(19:21:23), inc. in each of next 2 sts., k.16, inc. in each of next 2 sts., k.6(7:8:9). [77(81:85:89) sts.]
Next row: p.
Next row: k.7(8:9:10), inc. in each of next 2 sts., k.18, inc. in each of next 2 sts., k.19(21:23:25), inc. in each of next 2 sts., k.18, inc. in each of next 2 sts., k.7(8:9:10). [85(89:93:97) sts.]
Next row: p.
Next row: k.8(9:10:11), inc. in each of next 2 sts., k.20, inc. in each of next 2 sts., k.21(23:25:27), inc. in each of next 2 sts., k.20, inc. in each of next 2 sts., k.8(9:10:11). [93(97:101:105) sts.]
Cast off purlwise.

MAKING UP

Press work lightly on wrong side.
Sew up side and sleeve seams.
Set in sleeves, gathering in excess fullness at top of sleeve head.
Fold neck border in half to wrong side at ridge and sl.-hem loosely in position all round.
Catch down cast-on sts. of borders to main work.
Press all seams.
Sew on buttons.

Three-colour Norwegian Twin Set   *1959*

Stocking stitch twinset with allover Norwegian design, cardigan with patterned collar, all with ribbed welts

★★★   Suitable for experienced knitters

MATERIALS

Yarn
Pingouin Pingolaine
5(5:5:6:6) × 50g. balls Main Col. A
1(1:1:1:1) × 50g. ball Col. B
1(1:1:1:1) × 50g. ball Col. C

Needles
1 pair 2¾mm.
1 pair 3¼mm.
1 crochet hook 2.5mm.

Buttons
5(6:6:6:6)

MEASUREMENTS

Chest
54(56:59:61:64) cm.
21(22:23:24:25) in.
1/2(2:3:4:5) approx. age

Length
Sweater:
35(38:40:42:45) cm.
13¾(15:15¾:16½:17) in.
Cardigan:
37(40:42:44:47) cm.
14½(15¾:16½:17¼:18½) in.

Sleeve Seam
Sweater:
23(25:27:28:30) cm.
9(9¾:10½:11:11¾) in.
Cardigan:
24(26:28:29:31) cm.
9½(10¼:11:11¼:12¼) in.

TENSION

28 sts. and 32 rows = 10 cm. (4 in.) square

over patt. on 3¼mm. needles. If your tension square does not correspond to these measurements, adjust the needle size used.

ABBREVIATIONS

k = knit; p. = purl; st(s). = stitch(es); inc. = increase(ing); dec. = decreas(ing); beg. = begin(ning); rem. = remain(ing); rep. = repeat; alt. = alternate; tog. = together; sl. = slip (transfer one stitch from left needle, knitwise unless otherwise stated, to right hand needle.); cont. = continue; patt. = pattern; foll. = following; folls. = follows; mm. = millimetres; cm. = centimetres; in. = inches; st. st. = stocking st.: one row k., one row p.; g. st. = garter st.: every row k.; incs. = increases; decs. = decreases; d.c. = double crochet ; ch. = chain st.

SWEATER BACK

Cast on 76(84:90:98:104) sts. with 2¾mm. needles and A.
Work 5 cm. (2 in.) in k.1, p.1 rib, inc. 1 st. at beg. of last row. [77(85:91:99:105) sts.]
Change to 3¼mm. needles and st. st.
Work in patt. from chart 1, reading from 1(2:3:4:5) to dotted line, working st. to

Chart 1

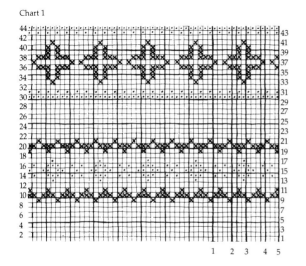

1 2 3 4 5

☐ = Col A
☒ = Col B
☑ = Col C

Chart 2

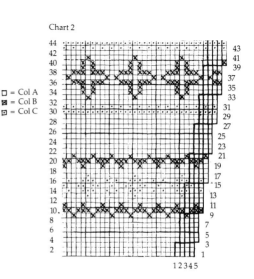

1 2 3 4 5

left of dotted line (centre st.), and working from dotted line back to 1(2:3:4:5). These 44 rows form the patt. which is rep. throughout.
Work until back measures 23(25:27:28:30) cm. (9(9¾:10½:11:11¾) in.), ending with a wrong side row.

Shape Armholes

Cast off 3(3:4:4:5) sts. at beg. of next 2 rows.
Dec. 1 st. at each end of next 2 right side rows. [67(75:79:87:91) sts.]
Work straight until armholes measure 12(13:13:14:15) cm. (4¾(5:5:5½:5¾) in.), ending with a wrong side row.

Shape Shoulders

Cast off 4(4:5:5:5) sts. at beg. of next 2 rows.
Cast off 4(5:5:5:6) sts. at beg. of next 2 rows.
Cast off 5(5:5:6:6) sts. at beg. of next 2 rows.
Cast off 5(5:6:6:6) sts. at beg. of next 2 rows.
Leave rem. 31(37:37:43:45) sts. on holder.

SWEATER FRONT

Work as for back until armholes measure 7(8:8:9:10) cm. (2¾(3¼:3¼:3½:4) in.), ending with a wrong side row.

Shape Neck

1st row: patt. 22(23:25:28:29), turn.
Work left side on these sts., leaving rem. sts. on holder.
** Keeping patt. straight, dec. 1 st. at neck edge on every right side row until 18(19:21:22:23) sts. rem.
Work straight until armhole matches back to shoulder, ending at armhole edge.

Shape Shoulder

Cast off 4(4:5:5:5) sts. at beg. of next row.
Work 1 row.
Cast off 4(5:5:5:6) sts. at beg. of next row.
Work 1 row.
Cast off 5(5:5:6:6) sts. at beg. of next row.
Work 1 row.
Cast off rem. 5(5:6:6:6) sts. **
With right side of front. sts. facing, sl. centre 23(29:29:31:33) sts. onto holder.
1st row: rejoin yarn to neck edge of rem. 22(23:25:28:29) sts., patt. to end.
Work as for left side from ** to **.

SLEEVES

Cast on 46(48:50:52:54) sts. with 2¾mm. needles and A.
Work 5 cm. (2 in.) in k.1, p.1 rib, inc. 1 st. at beg. of last row. [47(49:51:53:55) sts.]
Change to 3¼mm. needles and st. st.
Work in patt. from chart 2, inc. 1 st. at each end of 4th row and every foll. 6th row until there are 63(65:67:69:71) sts., working inc. sts. into patt.
Work straight until sleeve measures same length as back to armholes, ending with same patt. row as back to match patt. stripes.

Shape Top

Cast off 3(3:4:4:5) sts. at beg. of next 2 rows.
Dec. 1 st. at each end of every right side row until 35(35:37:37:37) sts. rem.
Work 1 row.
Cast off 3 sts. at beg. of next 4 rows.
Cast off rem. sts.

NECKBAND

Sew up left shoulder seam.
With A and 2¾mm. needles and right side facing, k. across 31(37:37:43:45) sts. from back holder, k. up 19 sts. from left side, k. across 23(29:29:31:33) sts. from front holder and k. up 19 sts. up other side of neck. [92(104:104:112:116) sts.]
Work 3 cm. (1¼ in.) in k.1, p.1 rib.
Cast off loosely in rib.

CARDIGAN BACK

Work as for sweater back, making sides 1 cm. (½ in.) longer, and armholes 1 cm. (½ in.) longer.

CARDIGAN LEFT FRONT

Cast on 39(43:46:50:53) sts. with 2¾mm. needles and A.
Work 5 cm. (2 in.) in k.1, p.1 rib, beg. alt. rows p.1 on 1st, 2nd and 5th sizes only.
Change to 3¼mm. needles and st. st.
Work from chart 1, reading from 1(2:3:4:5) to sts. beyond dotted line on k. rows, then on p. rows reading from left to right, work st. before dotted line, then work to 1(2:3:4:5).
Work until front matches back to armhole, ending at side edge.

Shape Armhole

Cast off 3(3:4:4:5) sts. at beg. of next row.
Dec. 1 st. at armhole edge on next 2 right side rows. [34(38:40:44:46) sts.]
Work straight until armhole measures 3 cm. (1¼ in.) less than cardigan back to shoulder, ending at centre front.

Shape Neck

Next row: cast off 10(10:10:10:11) sts., patt. to end.
Work 1 row.
Cast off 2(3:3:4:4) sts. at neck edge on next and foll. 2 alt. rows. [18(19:21:22:23) sts.]
Work straight until armhole measures same as cardigan back to shoulder, ending at armhole edge.

Shape Shoulder

Work as for sweater front shoulder.

CARDIGAN RIGHT FRONT

Work as for cardigan left front, reading patt. chart from st. before dotted line to 1(2:3:4:5) on k. rows, and in reverse on p. rows.

SLEEVES

Cast on 48(50:52:54:56) sts. with 2¾r.m. needles and A.

Work 5 cm. (2 in.) in k.1, p.1 rib, inc. 1 st. on last row. [49(51:53:55:57) sts.]
Change to 3¼mm. needles and st. st.
Work in patt. from chart 2, noting that there is 1 more st. at each side, therefore reading from 1 st. before 1(2:3:4:5) to dotted line, working centre and reading from dotted line to 1 st. after 1(2:3:4:5), AT THE SAME TIME inc. 1 st. at each end of 4th row and every foll. 6th row until there are 65(67:69:71:73) sts., working inc. sts. into patt.
Work straight until sleeve measures same length as back to armholes, ending with same patt. 'row as back to match patt. stripes.

Shape Top

Cast off 3(3:4:4:5) sts. at beg. of next 2 rows.
Dec. 1 st. at each end of every right side row until 35(35:37:37:37) sts. rem.
Cast off 2 sts. at beg. of next 4 rows.
Cast off rem. sts.

NECKBAND

Sew up both shoulder seams.
With A, 2¾mm. needles and right side facing, k. up 24(27:28:29:30) sts. up right front neck, k. across of back neck, then k. up 24(27:28:29:30) sts. down left front neck. [79(91:93:101:105) sts.]
Work 3 cm. (1¼ in.) in k.1, p.1 rib.
Cast off loosely in rib.

MAKING UP

Sweater

Sew up right shoulder and neckband seam.
Set in sleeves.
Sew up side and sleeve seams.

Cardigan

Set in sleeves.
Sew up side and sleeve seams.

Button Band

With right side facing and A, work 6 rows in d.c. along front edge, left side for girl and right side for boy.

Mark positions for buttons, first to come 1 cm. (½ in.) from lower edge and last to come 1 cm. (½ in.) from top edge, with remainder spaced evenly between.
Sew on buttons.

Buttonhole Band

With right side facing and A, work 3 rows in d.c.
Next row: work across, missing 2 d.c. at position for each buttonhole and working 2 ch. in their place.
Next row: work across, working 2 d.c. into each set of 2 ch.
Work 1 more row.
Press both garments under a damp cloth with a warm iron, omitting ribbing.

Diagonal-stitch Cardigan

*V-neck cardigan in diagonal stitch, with set-in sleeves,
two knitted-in pockets and moss stitch borders*

★ Suitable for beginners

NB Garment was photographed without buttons.

MATERIALS

Yarn
Christian de Falbe Studio Yarns
Watership
4(4:5:6) × 20g. balls

Needles
1 pair 2¾mm.
1 pair 3¾mm.

Buttons
4

MEASUREMENTS

Chest
46(51:56:61) cm.
18(20:22:24) in.
6 months/1(1/2:2/3:4/5) approx. age

Length
25(28:31:36) cm.
9¾(11:12¼:14) in.

Sleeve Seam
15(18:21:27) cm.
5¾(7:8¼:10½) in.

TENSION

25 sts. and 36 rows = 10 cm. (4 in.) square over patt. on 3¾mm. needles. If your tension square does not correspond to these measurements, adjust the needle size used.

ABBREVIATIONS

k. = knit; p. = purl; st(s). = stitch(es); inc. = increas(ing); dec. = decreas(ing); beg. = begin(ning); rem. = remain(ing); rep. = repeat; alt. = alternate; tog. = together; sl. = slip (transfer one stitch from left needle, knitwise unless otherwise stated, to right hand needle.); cont. = continue; patt. = pattern; foll. = following; folls. = follows; mm. = millimetres; cm. = centimetres; in. = inches; st. st. = stocking st.: one row k., one row p.; g. st. = garter st.: every row k.; incs. = increases; decs. = decreases.

BACK

Cast on 65(70:75:80) sts. with 2¾mm. needles.
1st row: * k.1, p.1, rep. from * to last 1(0:1:0) st., k.1(0:1:0) st.
2nd row: k.1(0:1:0) st., * p.1, k.1, rep. from * to end.
These 2 rows form moss st. patt.
Rep. 1st and 2nd rows 3 times.
Change to 3¾mm. needles and patt. as folls.:
1st row (right side): * k.3, p.2, rep. from * to end.
2nd row: * p.1, k.2, p.2, rep. from * to end.
3rd row: * k.1, p.2, k.2, rep. from * to end.
4th row: * p.3, k.2, rep. from * to end.
5th row: * p.1, k.3, p.1, rep. from * to end.
6th row: * k.2, p.3, rep. from * to end.
7th row: * k.2, p.2, k.1, rep. from * to end.

8th row: * p.2, k.2, p.1, rep. from * to end.
9th row: * p.2, k.3, rep. from * to end.
10th row: * k.1, p.3, k.1, rep. from * to end.
These 10 rows form patt.
Cont. in patt. until work measures 14(15:17:19) cm. (5½(5¾:6½:7½) in.).

Shape Armholes
Cast off 2(2:2:3) sts. at beg. of next 2 rows.
Dec. 1 st. at each end of next and every foll. alt. row until 53(58:61:64) sts. rem.
Cont. without shaping until work measures 25(28:31:36) cm. (9¾(11: 12¼:14) in.).

Shape Shoulders
Cast off 4(5:5:5) sts. at beg. of next 2 rows.
Cast off 5 sts. at beg. of next 2 rows.
Cast off 5(5:5:6) sts. at beg. of next 2 rows.
Cast off rem. 25(28:31:32) sts.

LEFT FRONT

Cast on 31(33:35:37) sts. with 2¾mm. needles.
Work 8 rows in moss st. as for 1st size of back.
Change to 3¾mm. needles and work as folls.:
1st row: * k.3, p.2, rep. from * to last 1(3:0:2) sts., k.1(3:0:2).
2nd row: k.0(1:0:0), p.1(2:0:2), * p.1, k.2, p.2, rep. from * to end.
3rd row: * k.1, p.2, k.2, rep. from * to last 1(3:0:2) sts., k.1(1:0:1), p.0(2:0:1).
4th row: p.0(1:0:0), k.1(2:0:2), * p.3, k.2, rep. from * to end.
These 4 rows set patt.

Cont. in patt. to match back until work measures same as back to armholes, ending with a wrong side row.

Shape Armhole and V-neck

1st row: cast off 2(2:2:3) sts., patt. to last 2 sts., k.2 tog.

Dec. 1 st. at each end of next 4(4:5:5) alt. rows.

Dec. 1 st. at neck edge only on every foll. 2nd(2nd:2nd:3rd) row until 14(15:15:16) sts. rem.

Cont. without shaping until work measures same as back to shoulders.

Shape Shoulder

Cast off 4(5:5:5) sts. at beg. of next row.
Work 1 row.
Cast off 5 sts. at beg. of next row.
Work 1 row.
Cast off rem. 5(5:5:6) sts.

RIGHT FRONT

Work as for left front, reversing all shapings.

SLEEVES

Cast on 40(40:40:40) sts. with 2¾mm. needles.

Work 8 rows in moss st. as folls.:

1st row: * k.1, p.1, rep. from * to end.
2nd row: * p.1, k.1, rep. from * to end.

Change to 3¾mm. needles and work in patt. as for back, inc. 1 st. at each end of every 5th row until there are 52(54:56:60) sts., working extra sts. into patt.

Cont. without shaping until work measures 15(18:21:27) cm. (5¾(7:8¼: 10½) in.).

Shape Top

Cast off 2(2:2:3) sts. at beg. of next 2 rows.
Dec. 1 st. at each end of next and every foll. alt. row until 34 sts. rem.
Cast off 6 sts. at beg. of next 2 rows.
Cast off.

FRONT BAND

Sew up shoulder seams.

Cast on 7 sts. with 2¾mm. needles.

Work 4 rows in moss st. as given for 1st size at beg. of back.

5th row: moss st. 3, cast off 1 st., moss st. to end.

6th row: moss st. 3, cast on 1 st., moss st. 3.

Cont. in moss st., making 3 further buttonholes as on 5th and 6th rows at the foll. intervals:

1st size: 5,9,13 cm. (2,3½,5 in.).
2nd size: 6,10,15 cm. (2¼,4,5¾ in.).
3rd size: 6,11,17 cm. (2¼,4¼,6½ in.).
4th size: 7,13,19 cm. (2¾,5,7½ in.).

Cont. in moss st., sewing band onto fronts gradually, until band fits all around front edge when slightly stretched.

Cast off.

MAKING UP

Sew up side and sleeve seams.
Set in sleeves.
Sew on buttons.

Lacy-yoked Sweater

*Long-sleeved sweater with dropped shoulderline, squared neck,
triangular lacy sections on yoke and shoulder buttoning*

★ Suitable for beginners

MATERIALS

Yarn
Wendy Ascot 4 ply
2(3) × 50g. balls

Needles
1 pair 3mm.
1 pair 3¼mm.

Buttons
2

MEASUREMENTS

Chest
46(51) cm.
18(20) in.
6 months/1(1/2) approx. age

Length
24(27) cm.
9½(10½) in.

Sleeve Seam
15(19) cm.
5¾(7½) in.

TENSION

28 sts. and 36 rows = 10 cm. (4 in.) square over st. st. on 3¼mm. needles. If your tension square does not correspond to these measurements, adjust the needle size used.

ABBREVIATIONS

k. = knit; p. = purl; st(s). = stitch(es); inc. = increas(ing); dec. = decreas(ing); beg. = begin(ning); rem. = remain(ing); rep. = repeat; alt. = alternate; tog. = together; sl. = slip (transfer one stitch from left needle, knitwise unless otherwise stated, to right hand needle.); cont. = continue; patt. = pattern; foll. = following; folls. = follows; mm. = millimetres; cm.' = centimetres; in. = inches; st. st. = stocking st.: one row k., one row p.; g. st. = garter st.: every row k.; incs. = increases; decs. = decreases; y.fwd. = yarn forward.

BACK

Cast on 68(76) sts. with 3mm. needles.
Work 3 cm. (1¼ in.) in k.2, p.2 rib.
Change to 3¼mm. needles.
Beg. with a k. row, work straight in st. st. until work measures 15(17) cm. (5¾(6½) in.) from cast-on edge, ending with a p. row.

Shape Armholes
Cast off 4 sts. at beg. of next 2 rows. [60(68) sts.]
Cont. straight in st. st. until armholes measure 5 cm. (2 in.), ending with a p. row.
Now work triangle patt. as folls.:
1st row (right side): k.8(9), * y.fwd., k.2 tog., k.12(14), rep. from * twice, y.fwd., k.2 tog., k.8(9).
2nd row and all even rows: p.
3rd row: k.7(8), * (y.fwd., k.2 tog.) twice, k.10(12), rep. from * twice, (y.fwd., k.2 tog.) twice, k.7(8).

5th row: k.6(7), * (y.fwd., k.2 tog.) 3 times, k.8(10), rep. from * twice, (y.fwd., k.2 tog.) 3 times, k.6(7).
7th row: k.5(6), * (y.fwd., k.2 tog.) 4 times, k.6(8), rep. from * twice, (y.fwd., k.2 tog.) 4 times, k.5(6).
9th row: k.4(5), * (y.fwd., k.2 tog.) 5 times, k.4(6), rep. from * twice, (y.fwd., k.2 tog.) 5 times, k.4(5).
11th row: k.3(4), * (y.fwd., k.2 tog.) 6 times, k.2(4), rep. from * twice, (y.fwd., k.2 tog.) 6 times, k.3(4).
1st size only:
P.1 row.
13th row: k.2, * y.fwd., k.2 tog., rep. from * to end.
K. 5 rows.
Cast off.
2nd size only:
P. 1 row.
13th row: k.3, * (y.fwd., k.2 tog.) 7 times, k.2, rep. from * twice, (y.fwd., k.2 tog.) 7 times, k.3.
P. 1 row.
15th row: k.2, * y.fwd., k.2 tog., rep. from * to end.
K. 5 rows.
Cast off.

FRONT

Work as for back until end of armhole shaping. [60(68) sts.]
Work 2(0) rows straight.
Now work triangle patt. as folls.:
1st row (right side): k.22(25), y.fwd., k.2 tog., k.12(14), y.fwd., k.2 tog., k.22(25).
2nd row: p.

3rd row: k.21(24), (y.fwd., k.2 tog.) twice, k.10(12), (y.fwd., k.2 tog.) twice, k.21(24).
4th row: p.
These 4 rows set patt.
Cont. to work these 2 centre triangles, keeping the rest of the front in st. st. until rows 12(14) have been worked.
Next row: k.16(18), (y.fwd., k.2 tog.) 14(16) times, k.16(18).
Next row: p.16(18), k.28(32), p.16(18).
Now work triangles on shoulders as folls.:
1st row: k.8(9), y.fwd., k.2 tog., k.40(46), y.fwd., k.2 tog., k.8(9).
2nd row: p.16(18), k.28(32), p.16(18).
3rd row: k.7(8), (y.fwd., k.2 tog.) twice, k.38(44), (y.fwd., k.2 tog.) twice, k.7(8).
4th row: as 2nd.

Shape Neck
Next row: patt. 20(22) sts. and leave on holder until required, cast off next 20(24) sts., then patt. to end. [20(22) sts.]
Cont. on these last 20(22) sts.
Keeping the 4 sts. at neck edge in g. st., patt. 8(10) more rows.
K. 5 rows.
Cast off.
Rejoin yarn to wrong side of rem. 20(22) sts. and work as for first side to end.

SLEEVES

Beg. at top edge.
Cast on 60(64) sts. with 3¼mm. needles.
P. 1 row.
Now work in patt. as folls.:
1st row: k.23(24), (y.fwd., k.2 tog.) 7(8) times, k.23(24).
2nd and all even rows: p.
3rd row: k.24(25), (y.fwd., k.2 tog.) 6(7) times, k.24(25).
5th row: k.25(26), (y.fwd., k.2 tog.) 5(6) times, k.25(26).
7th row: k.26(27), (y.fwd., k.2 tog.) 4(5) times, K.26(27).
9th row: k.27(28), (y.fwd., k.2 tog.) 3(4) times, k.27(28).
11th row: k.28(29), (y.fwd., k.2 tog.) 2(3) times, k.28(29).
13th row: k.29(30), (y.fwd., k.2 tog.) once (twice), k.29(30).
2nd size only:
15th row: k.31, y.fwd., k.2 tog., k.31.
Both sizes:
Beg. with a p. row, work straight in st. st. until work measures 13(17) cm. (5(6½) in.).
Dec. row: k.0(2), * k.1, k.2 tog., rep. from * 19 times, k.0(2). [40(44) sts.]
Change to 3mm. needles.
Work 3 cm. (1¼ in.) in k.2, p.2 rib.
Cast off loosely in rib.

MAKING UP

Sew up shoulder seams for 3 cm. (1¼ in.) from shoulder edges.
Set in sleeves, sewing last 5 rows of sides of sleeves to cast-off sts. of armhole shaping.
Sew up side and sleeve seams.
Make buttonloop on each front shoulder.
Sew a button to each back shoulder to correspond.

Two-colour Zig-zag Cardigan

1961

Chevron-pattern cardigan with round neck, raglan sleeves and ribbed borders with turnback cuffs

★★ Suitable for knitters with some previous experience

MATERIALS

Yarn
Patons Clansman 4 ply
2(2:3:3:4) × 50g. balls Main Col. A
2(2:2:3:3) × 50g. balls Col. B

Needles
1 pair 2¾mm.
1 pair 3¼mm.

Buttons
6(6:6:7:7)

MEASUREMENTS

Chest
46(51:56:61:66) cm.
18(20:22:24:26) in.
6 months/1(1/2:2/3:4/5:6/7) approx. age

Length
32(37:40:44:47) cm.
12½(14½:15¾:17¼:18½) in.

Sleeve Seam
20(23:25:28:30) cm.
7¾(9:9¾:11:11¾) in.

TENSION

32 sts. and 32 rows = 10 cm. (4 in.) square over patt. on 3¼mm. needles. If your tension square does not correspond to these measurements, adjust the needle size used.

ABBREVIATIONS

k. = knit; p. = purl; st(s). = stitch(es); inc. = increas(ing); dec. = decreas(ing); beg. = begin(ning); rem. = remain(ing); rep. = repeat; alt. = alternate; tog. = together; sl. = slip (transfer one stitch from left needle, knitwise unless otherwise stated, to right hand needle.); cont. = continue; patt. = pattern; foll. = following; folls. = follows; mm. = millimetres; cm. = centimetres; in. = inches; st. st. = stocking st.: one row k., one row p.; g. st. = garter st.: every row k.; incs. = increases; decs. = decreases; t.b.l. = through back of loops; m.1 = make 1 st.: pick up horizontal loop lying before next st. and work into back of it.

BACK

Cast on 61(69:77:85:93) sts. with 2¾mm. needles and A.
1st row (right side): k.1 t.b.l., * p.1, k.1 t.b.l., rep. from * to end.

2nd row: p.1 t.b.l., * k.1, p.1 t.b.l., rep. from * to end.
Rep. last 2 rows 6(6:7:7:8) times more, then 1st row again.
Next row: rib 3(7:2:6:1), m.1, * rib 3(3:4:4:5), m.1, rep. from * to last 4(8:3:7:2) sts., rib 4(8:3:7:2). [80(88:96:104:112) sts.]
Join in B, change to 3¼mm. needles and st. st.
Work in zig-zag patt. as folls.:
1st row (right side): k. * 2A, 2B, rep. from * to end.
2nd row: p. 1B, * 2A, 2B, rep. from * to last 3 sts., 2A, 1B.
3rd row: k. * 2B, 2A, rep. from * to end.
4th row: p. 1A, * 2B, 2A, rep. from * to last 3 sts., 2B, 1A.
5th row: as 3rd.
6th row: as 2nd.
These 6 rows form patt.
Work straight in patt. until back measures 20(23:25:28:30) cm. (7¾(9:9¾: 11:11¾) in.) from beg., ending with a wrong side row.

Shape Raglans
Cast off 4 sts. at beg. of next 2 rows.
Dec. 1 st. at each end of every row until 68(72:76:80:84) sts. rem.
Patt. 1 row.
Now dec. 1 st. at each end of next and every alt. row until 32(34:36:38:40) sts. rem.
Patt. 1 row.
Cast off in patt.

LEFT FRONT

Cast on 29(33:37:41:45) sts. with 2¾mm. needles and A.
Work 15(15:17:17:19) rows in twisted rib as given for back.
Next row: rib 4(1:3:5:2) sts., m.1, * rib 2(3:3:3:4), m.1, rep. from * to last 5(2:4: 6:3) sts., rib 5(2:4:6:3) sts. [40(44:48:52:56) sts.].

Join in B.
Change to 3¼mm. needles and beg. with a 1st row.
Work straight in zig-zag patt. as given for back until front matches back at side edge, ending with a wrong side row.

Shape Raglan
Cast off 4 sts. at beg. of next row.
Work 1 row straight.
Now dec. 1 st. at raglan edge on every row until 34(36:38:40:42) sts. rem.
Now dec. 1 st. at raglan edge on next and every alt. row until 23(24:25:26:27) sts. rem.

Shape Neck
With wrong side facing, cast off 7(8:9: 10:11) sts. at beg. of next row.
Cont. dec. at raglan edge on every alt. row, and at the same time dec. 1 st. at neck edge on every row until 5 sts. rem.
Now keep neck edge straight and cont. dec. at raglan edge on alt. rows as before until 2 sts. rem.
Next row: patt. 2, turn, k.2 tog.
Fasten off.

RIGHT FRONT

Work to match left front, reversing all shapings.

SLEEVES

Cast on 37(39:43:45:49) sts. with 2¾mm. needles and A.
Work 15(15:17:17:19) rows in twisted rib as for back.
Next row: rib 3(1:3:1:3), m.1, * rib 3, m.1, rep. from * to last 4(2:4:2:4) sts., rib

4(2:4:2:4) sts. [48(52:56:60:64) sts.]
Join in B, change to 3¼mm. needles.
Beg. with a 1st row, work in zig-zag patt.
as for back.
Shape sides by inc. 1 st. at each end of
1st(7th:1st:7th:1st) row, and every foll.
6th(6th:8th:8th:10th) row until there are
64(68:72:76:80) sts., taking inc. sts. into
patt.
Work straight until sleeve seam measures
20(23:25:28:30) cm. (7¾(9:9¾:11:11¾)
in.), ending with a wrong side row.

Shape Raglans
Cast off 4 sts. at beg. of next 2 rows.
Dec. 1 st. at each end of every row until
28(32:36:40:44) sts. rem.
Now dec. on next and every alt. row until
4 sts. rem., ending with a p. row.
Cast off in patt.

FRONT BORDERS

Left Border
Cast on 9 sts. with 2¾mm. needles and
A.
1st row (right side): k.2 t.b.l., * p.1, k.1
t.b.l., rep. from * to last st., k.1 t.b.l.
2nd row: k.1, * p.1 t.b.l., k.1, rep. from * to
end.
Rep. last 2 rows until strip fits up left
front to beg. of neck shaping when
slightly stretched, ending with a wrong
side row.
Sew border in position as working, to
ensure a good fit.
Leave sts. on safety pin at top.

Right Border
Work to match left border, with the
addition of 5(5:5:6:6) buttonholes, first to
come 2 cm. (¾ in.) above beg. of border,
last to come 4 cm. (1½ in.) below beg. of
neck shaping, with rest spaced evenly
between.
Mark position of buttons on left border
with pins before working buttonholes.
1st buttonhole row: rib 3, cast off 3, rib to
end.
2nd row: work back in rib, casting on 3
sts. over those cast off.

NECK BORDER

Sew up raglan seams.
With right side facing, 2¾mm. needles
and A, rib 9 sts. from right border, pick
and up and k. 19(20:21:22:23) sts. up right
side of neck, 3 sts. from right sleeve top,
29(31:33:35:37) sts. from back, 3 sts. from
left sleeve top, 19(20:21:22:23) sts. down
left side, rib 9 sts. from left border.
[91(95:99:103:107) sts.].
Beg. with a 2nd row, work 3 rows in
twisted rib as for left border.
Make a buttonhole in next 2 rows.
Work another 3 rows in rib.
Cast off in rib.

MAKING UP

Press work lightly on wrong side, omit-
ting ribbing.
Sew up side and sleeve seams.
Press all seams.
Sew on buttons.

Fisherman's-rib, Round-neck Sweater 1982

Traditional fisherman's-ribbed sweater with round neck, raglan sleeves and ribbed welts

★★ Suitable for knitters with some previous experience

MATERIALS

Yarn
Sunbeam Pure New Wool 4 ply
4(5:5:6) × 50g. balls

Needles
1 pair 2¾mm.
1 pair 3¼mm.

MEASUREMENTS

Chest
51(56:61:66) cm.
20(22:24:26) in.
1(2/3:4/5:6/7) approx. age

Length
33(38:42:46) cm.
13(15:16½:18) in.

Sleeve Seam
21(23:27:31) cm.
8¼(9:10½:12¼) in.

TENSION

26 sts. and 52 rows = 10 cm. (4 in.) square over patt. on 3¼mm. needles. If your tension square does not correspond to these measurements, adjust the needle size used.

ABBREVIATIONS

k. = knit; p. = purl; st(s). = stitch(es); inc. = increas(ing); dec. = decreas(ing); beg. = begin(ning); rem. = remain(ing); rep. = repeat; alt. = alternate; tog. = together; sl. = slip (transfer one stitch from left needle, knitwise unless otherwise stated, to right hand needle.); cont. = continue; patt. = pattern; foll. = following; folls. = follows; mm. = millimetres; cm. = centimetres; in. = inches; st. st. = stocking st.: one row k., one row p.; g. st. = garter st.: every row k.; incs. = increases; decs. = decreases; p.s.s.o. = pass the sl. st. over; k.1b. = k. 1 below: k. into next st. one row below, at the same time sl. off st. above.

BACK

** Cast on 73(79:85:91) sts. with 2¾mm. needles.
1st row: k.2, * p.1, k.1, rep. from * to last st., k.1.
2nd row: * k.1, p.1, rep. from * to last st., k.1.
Rep. 1st and 2nd rows 6(8:10:12) times more.

Change to 3¼mm. needles and patt.
1st row (right side): k.
2nd row: k.1, * p.1, k.1b., rep. from * to last 2 sts., p.1, k.1.
These 2 rows form patt.
Work until back measures 22(25:28:31) cm. (8½(9¾:11:12¼) in.) from beg., ending with a wrong side row.
Mark each end of last row to indicate start of armholes.

Shape Raglans
1st row: k.3, sl.1, k.2 tog., p.s.s.o., k. to last 6 sts., k.3 tog., k.3.
2nd to 4th rows: work in patt.
5th row: as 1st.
Work 5 rows. **
Cont. dec. in this way at each end of next row and every foll. 6th row until 37(39: 41:43) sts. rem., and then every 4th row until 25(27:29:31) sts. rem.
Work 3 rows.
Cast off.

FRONT

Work as for back from ** to **.
Cont. dec. in this way at each end of next row and every foll. 6th row until 41(43:45: 47) sts. rem.
Work 4(4:2:2) rows.

Shape Neck
Next row: patt. 16(16:17:17) sts., cast off 9(11:11:13) sts., patt. to end.
Cont. on last set of sts.
3rd and 4th sizes only:
Next row: k.
Next row: k.2 tog., patt. to end.
All sizes:
Next row: k.3, sl.1, k.2 tog., p.s.s.o., k. to end.
Now dec. for raglan on 2 foll. 6th rows, AND AT THE SAME TIME dec. 1 st. at neck edge on next row, and then every alt. row until 3 sts. rem.
Work 1 row.
Next row: k.2 tog., k.1.
Next row: k.2 tog., fasten off.
Rejoin yarn to rem. sts. at neck edge and complete to match first side.

SLEEVES

Cast on 39(43:43:47) sts. with 2¾mm. needles.
Work 14(18:22:26) rows in rib as back.
Change to 3¼mm. needles and patt.
Work 6 rows.
Inc. 1 st. at each end of next row, and then every 10th row until there are 55(59:63:67) sts., working inc. sts. into patt.
Work until sleeve measures 21(23:27:31)

cm. (8¼(9:10½:12¼) in.) from beg., ending with a wrong side row.
Mark each end of last row to indicate start of sleeve top.

Shape Top
1st row: k.3, sl.1, k.2 tog., p.s.s.o., k. to last 6 sts., k.3 tog., k.3.
2nd to 4th rows: work in patt.
5th row: as 1st.
Work 5 rows.
Cont. to dec. in this way at each end of next row and every foll. 6th row until 11 sts. rem.
Work 3 rows.
Cast off.

NECK BORDER

Press each piece lightly.
Sew up front and right back raglan seams.
With 2¾mm. needles and right side facing, k. up to 13 sts. evenly along left sleeve top, 14(14:15:15) sts. down left side of neck, 9(11:11:13) sts. from the cast off sts., 14(14:15:15) sts. up right side of neck, 12 sts. along right sleeve top, and 30(32:34:36) sts. evenly along back neck edge.
1st-4th rows: k.
Now work 8 rows in k.1, p.1, rib.
Cast off in rib.

MAKING UP

Sew up left back raglan and neck border seam.
Sew up side and sleeve seams.
Press seams lightly.

Lacy, Flower-pattern Dress

Allover-patterned dress with gathered skirt, fitted yoke, puffed sleeves and back buttoning

★ Suitable for beginners

MATERIALS

Yarn
Pingouin Fil d'Ecosse No. 8
4(4) × 50g. balls

Needles
1 pair 2¾mm. for 1st size
1 pair 3mm. for 2nd size

Buttons
5

MEASUREMENTS

Chest
51(56) cm.
20(22) in.
1/2(2/3) approx. age

Length
43(51) cm.
16¾(20) in.

Sleeve Seam
5(6) cm.
2(2¼ in.)

TENSION

32 sts. and 44 rows = 10 cm. (4 in.) square over patt. on 2¾mm. needles.
30 sts. and 38 rows = 10 cm. (4 in.) square over patt. on 3mm. needles. If your tension does not correspond to these measurements, adjust the needle size used.

ABBREVIATIONS

k. = knit; p. = purl; st(s). = stitch(es); inc. = increas(ing); dec. = decreas(ing); beg. = begin(ning); rem. = remain(ing); rep. = repeat; alt. = alternate; tog. = together; sl. = slip (transfer one stitch from left needle, knitwise unless otherwise stated, to right hand needle.); cont. = continue; patt. = pattern; foll. = following; folls. = follows; mm. = millimetres; cm. = centimetres; in. = inches; st. st. = stocking st.: one row k., one row p.; g. st. = garter st.: every row k.; incs. = increases; decs. = decreases; y.fwd. = yarn forward; p.s.s.o. = pass the sl. st. over.

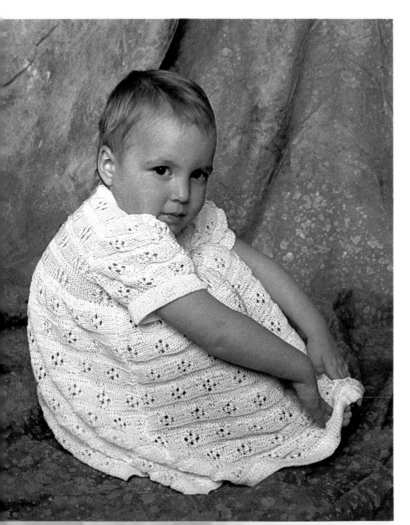

NB Use 2¾mm. needles for 1st size and 3mm. needles for 2nd size throughout.

FRONT

Cast on 166 sts.
Beg. with a k. row, work 20 rows in st. st. Fold up cast-on edge behind sts. on needle and work 1 st. from cast-on edge tog. with 1 st. from needle all along row to form hem.
Now work in patt. as folls.:
1st row (wrong side): k.
2nd row: p.
3rd row: k.1, * k.10, y.fwd., sl.1, k.1, p.s.s.o., rep. from * to last 9 sts., k.9.

4th row: p.

5th row: k.8, * sl.1, k.1, p.s.s.o., y.fwd., k.3, y.fwd., sl.1, k.1, p.s.s.o., k.5, rep. from * to last 2 sts., k.2.

6th row: p.

7th row: as 3rd.

8th row: p.

9th row: k.

10th row: k.

11th row: p.

12th to 14th rows: rep. 10th and 11th once, then work 10th again.

15th row: k.

16th row: p.

17th row: k.5, * y.fwd., sl.1, k.1, p.s.s.o., k.10, rep. from * to last 5 sts., y.fwd., sl.1, k.1, p.s.s.o., k.3.

18th row: p.

19th row: k.2, * sl.1, k.1, p.s.s.o., y.fwd., k.3, y.fwd., sl.1, k.1, p.s.s.o., k.5, rep. from * to last 8 sts., sl.1, k.1, p.s.s.o., y.fwd., k.3, y.fwd., sl.1, k.1, p.s.s.o., k.1.

20th row: p.

21st row: as 17th.

22nd row: p.

23rd and 24th rows: k.

25th row: p.

26th row: k.

27th and 28th rows: as 25th and 26th.

These 28 rows form patt.

Rep. these 28 rows 3 times more, then rows 1 to 13 again.

Dec. row: k.2 tog. all across row.

Next row: k., working 41st and 42nd sts. tog. [82 sts.] **

Work 13 rows in patt.

Shape Armholes

Cast off 3 sts. at beg. of next 2 rows.
Cont. in patt., dec. 1 st. at each end of every row until 68 sts. rem.
Cont. in patt. for a further 26 rows.

Shape Neck

Next row: patt. 26, cast off 16, patt. 26.
Work on last 26 sts. only as folls.:
Work 1 row.
Cont. in patt., casting off 2 sts. at beg. of next and foll. 3 alt. rows. [18 sts.]

Shape Shoulder

Cast off 9 sts. at beg. of next and foll. alt. row.
Cast off.
Rejoin yarn to rem. 26 sts. and work to match first side, reversing all shapings.

BACK

Work as for front to **

Divide for Opening

16th row: p.38, k.6, turn. (Last 6 sts. are centre back border and will be in g. st. to neck.)
Work 2 rows.
* *Next row*: k.2, cast off 2, k.2 including st. rem. on needle after casting off, work to end.
Next row: patt., casting on 2 sts. over those cast off.
Work 9 rows, thus ending at side edge.

Shape Armhole

Cast off 3 sts. at beg. of next row.
Working buttonholes on every 13th and 14th row from previous buttonhole, dec. 1 st. at armhole edge on next 4 rows. [37 sts.]
Cont. until a total of 4 buttonholes have been worked, thus ending at centre back edge.

Shape Neck

Cast off 10 sts. at beg. of next row and 3 sts. at beg. of foll. 3 alt. rows.

Shape Shoulder

Cast off 9 sts. at beg. of next and foll. alt. row.
Rejoin yarn to rem. sts. and cast on 6 sts. for border (keep these 6 sts. in g. st. throughout).
Complete to match first side, omitting buttonholes and reversing shapings.

SLEEVES

Cast on 55 sts.
Beg. with a k. row, work 20 rows in st. st.
Make a hem on next row as for front.
Inc. row: k.1, * inc. in next st., k.1, rep. from * to end. [82 sts.]
Beg. with a 2nd row, work 13 rows in patt.

Shape Top

Cast off 3 sts. at beg. of next 2 rows, then 1 st. at beg. of every row until 28 sts. rem.
Cast off, working k.2 tog. all across row at the same time.

NECKBAND

Sew up side, shoulder and sleeve seams.
Set in sleeves, gathering in fullness at the top.
Pick up and k. 19 sts. along left back neck, 36 sts. around front neck and 19 sts. along right back neck. [74 sts.]
Beg. with a p. row, work 3 rows in st. st.
* *Buttonhole row*: k. to last 4 sts., cast off 2, k. to end.
Next row: p.2, cast on 2 sts., p. to end. *
Work 4 rows.
Rep. from * to * once.
Work 3 rows.
Cast off VERY loosely.

MAKING UP

Fold neckband in half onto wrong side and hem so that the buttonholes correspond.
Buttonhole st. round buttonhole.
Sew down cast-on edge of button border neatly behind buttonhole border.
Sew on buttons.

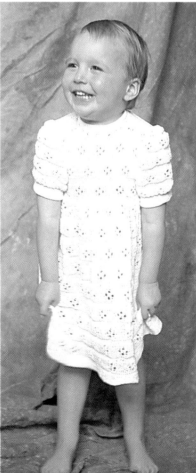

Twisted-stitch Slipover

Shaped, twisted-stitch sleeveless sweater with round neck and moss stitch bands, ribbed neck and hem

★ Suitable for beginners

MATERIALS

Yarn
Sunbeam St Ives 4 ply
5(5:6:6) × 25g. balls

Needles
1 pair 2¼mm.
1 pair 3mm.

Buttons
2

MEASUREMENTS

Chest
56(61:66:72) cm.
22(24:26:28) in.
2/3(4/5:6/7:8/9) approx. age

Length
34(38:42:46) cm.
13¼(15:16½:18) in.

TENSION

32 sts. and 36 rows = 10 cm. (4 in.) square over rib patt. (slightly stretched) on 3mm. needles. If your tension square does not correspond to these measurements, adjust the needle size used.

ABBREVIATIONS

k. = knit; p. = purl; st(s). = stitch(es); inc. = increas(ing); dec. = decreas(ing); beg. = begin(ning); rem. = remain(ing); rep. = repeat; alt. = alternate; tog. = together; sl. = slip (transfer one stitch from left needle, knitwise unless otherwise stated, to right hand needle.); cont. = continue; patt. = pattern; foll. = following; folls. = follows; mm. = millimetres; cm. = centimetres; in. = inches; st. st. = stocking st.: one row k., one row p.; g. st. = garter st.: every row k.; incs. = increases; decs. = decreases; Tw.2R = k. into front of 2nd st. on left hand needle, then k. into front of first st. on left hand needle and sl. both sts. off needle tog.

BACK

Cast on 90(98:106:114) sts. with 2¼mm. needles.
1st row: k.2, * p.2, k.2, rep. from * to end.
2nd row: p.2, * k.2, p.2, rep. from * to end.
Rep. these 2 rows for 5 cm. (2 in.), ending with a 2nd row and inc. 8(10:12:14) sts. evenly across last row. [98(108:118:128) sts.]

Change to 3mm. needles and cont. in patt. as folls.:
1st row (right side): p.1, k.1, p.1, * k.2, p.1, k.1, p.1, rep. from * to end.
2nd row: k.1, p.1, k.1, * p.2, k.1, p.1, k.1, rep. from * to end.
3rd row: p.1, k.1, p.1, * Tw.2R, p.1, k.1, p.1, rep. from * to end.
4th row: as 2nd.
These 4 rows form the patt. and are rep. throughout.
Cont. in patt. until work measures 20(22: 24:26) cm. (7¾(8½:9½:10¼) in.) from beg., ending with a wrong side row.

Shape Armholes

Keeping patt. straight, cast off 6(6:8:8) sts. at beg. of next 2 rows, 3 sts. at beg. of next 2 rows and 2 sts. at beg. of next 2 rows.
Now dec. 1 st. at each end of next and foll. 1(3:3:5) alt. rows. [72(78:84:90) sts.]
Cont. without shaping until armholes measure 14(16:18:20) cm. (5½(6¼:7:7¾) in.), ending with a wrong side row.

Shape Shoulders

Cast off 4(5:5:6) sts. at beg. of next 4 rows and 5(5:7:7) sts. at beg. of next 2 rows.
Cast off rem. 46(48:50:52) sts.

FRONT

Work as for back until armholes measure 9(11:11:12) cm. (3½(4¼:4¼:4¾) in.), ending with a wrong side row.

Shape Neck

Next row: patt. 31(33:36:38), turn and leave rem. sts. on spare needle.

Cast off 4 sts. at beg. of next row, 3 sts. at beg. of foll. 2 alt. rows and 2 sts. at beg. of foll. 2 alt. rows.
Cast off 1 st. at beg. of foll. 4(4:5:5) alt. rows. [13(15:17:19) sts.]
Cont. without shaping until armhole measures same as back, ending with a wrong side row.

Shape Shoulder

Cast off 4(5:5:6) sts. at beg. of next and foll. alt. row.
Work 1 row.
Cast off rem. 5(5:7:7) sts.
Return to sts. on spare needle, with right side facing rejoin yarn.
Next row: cast off 10(12:12:14) sts., patt. to end.
Work 1 row.
Cont. to match first side, reversing all shapings.

NECKBAND

Sew up right shoulder seam, then sew up left shoulder for about half its length, starting from armhole edge.
Cast on 9 sts. with 2¼mm. needles.
1st row: k.1, * p.1, k.1, rep. from * to end.
Rep. this row until band is long enough to fit round neck edge, when slightly stretched.
Cast off.

Armhole Bands

Work as for neckband, making bands long enough to fit round armholes, when slightly stretched.

MAKING UP

Press work very lightly taking care not to flatten the patt.
Sew on bands overlapping them slightly over the edge of work.
Sew up side seams.
Sew 2 buttons to left back shoulder and make loops on left front to correspond.
Press seams.

Flower-pattern, Fair Isle Sweater 1960

Three-colour Fair Isle sweater with round neck, long, set-in sleeves, shoulder opening for two smallest sizes, and ribbed welts

★ Suitable for adventurous beginners

MATERIALS

Yarn
Rowan Yarns Light Tweed
5(5:5:5:6) × 25g. hanks Main Col. A
2(2:2:2:3) × 25g. hanks Col. B
2(2:2:2:3) × 25g. hanks Col. C

Needles
1 pair 2¾mm.
1 pair 3¼mm.
st. holder

Buttons
1st and 2nd sizes only: 2

MEASUREMENTS

Chest
51(56:61:66:71) cm.
20(22:24:26:28) in.
1/2(2/3:4/5:6/7:8/9) approx. age

Length
26(31:37:42:47) cm.
10¼(12¼:14½:16½:18½) in.

Sleeve Seam
15(20:25:31:35) cm.
5¾(7¾:9¾:12¼:13¾) in.

TENSION

28 sts. and 36 rows = 10 cm. (4 in.) square over st. st. on 3¼mm. needles. If your tension square does not correspond to these measurements, adjust the needle size used.

ABBREVIATIONS

k. = knit; p. = purl; st(s). = stitch(es); inc. = increas(ing); dec. = decreas(ing); beg. = begin(ning); rem. = remain(ing); rep. = repeat; alt. = alternate; tog. = together; sl. = slip (transfer one stitch from left needle, knitwise unless otherwise stated, to right hand needle.); cont. = continue; patt. = pattern; foll. = following; folls. = follows; mm. = millimetres; cm. = centimetres; in. = inches; st. st. = stocking st.: one row k., one row p.; g. st. = garter st.: every row k.; incs. = increases; decs. = decreases.

BACK

Cast on 76(84:90:98:104) sts. with 2¾mm. needles and A.
Work in k.1, p.1 rib for 2 cm. (¾ in.), inc. 1 st. at end of last row. [77(85:91:99:105) sts.]
Change to 3¼mm. needles.
Joining in and breaking off colours as required, cont. in st. st., working in patt. from chart.
NB When working from chart, read odd rows k. from right to left and even rows p. from left to right.

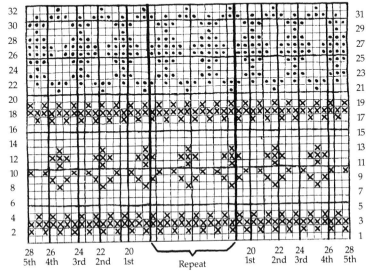

28 26 24 22 20   20 22 24 26 28
5th 4th 3rd 2nd 1st   Repeat   1st 2nd 3rd 4th 5th

□ = Col A
☒ = Col B
⊡ = Col C

Cont. until work measures 15(19:23:27:31) cm. (5¾(7½:9:10½:12¼) in.) from beg., ending with a p. row. [46(60:74:90:104) patt. rows]

Shape Armholes
Keeping patt. straight, cast off 4 sts. at the beg. of next 2 rows.
Now dec. 1 st. at each end of next row, and 0(1:2:3:3) foll. alt rows. [67(73:77:83:89) sts.]
** Cont. straight until armholes measure 11(12:14:15:16) cm. (4¼(4¾:5½:5¾:6¼) in.). [40(44:50:54:58) patt. rows from beg. of armhole shaping.]

Shape Shoulders
Cast off 9(10:11:12:13) sts. at beg. of next 2 rows.
Cast off 9(10:10:11:12) sts. at beg. of foll. 2 rows.
Sl. rem. 31(33:35:37:39) sts. onto holder.

FRONT

Work as for back to **.
Cont. straight until armholes measure 7(8:9:10:10) cm. (2¾(3¼:3½:4:4) in.), ending with a right side row. [25(29:31:35:35) patt. rows from beg. of armhole shaping.]

Shape Neck
Next row: patt. 26(28:30:33:35) sts., leave these sts. on a spare needle until required for right front shoulder, cast off 15(17:17:17:19) sts., work to end and cont. on these 26(28:30:33:35) sts. for left front shoulder.
Dec. 1 st. at neck edge on next 8(8:9:10:10) rows. [18(20:21:23:25) sts.]
Work 6(6:9:8:12) rows.

Shape Shoulder
Cast off 9(10:11:12:13) sts. at beg. of next row.
Work 1 row.
Cast off rem. 9(10:10:11:12) sts.
Cast off.

Right front shoulder:
With right side facing, rejoin yarn to inner edge of sts. left on spare needle.
Next row: dec. 1 st., work to end of row.
Work as for left front shoulder to end, but work 1 extra row before shaping shoulder.

SLEEVES

Cast on 48(48:48:54:54) sts. with 2¾mm. needles and A.
Work in k.1, p.1 rib for 2 cm. (¾ in.), inc. 1 st. at end of last row. [49(49:49:55:55) sts.]
Change to 3¼mm. needles.
Joining in and breaking off colours as required, cont. in st. st., working in patt. from chart as folls.:
1st size: beg. with the 1st patt. row, placing sts. as for 2nd size on chart.
2nd size: beg. with 2 rows A, then foll. chart from 1st row, placing sts. as for 2nd size on chart.
3rd size: beg. with 23rd patt. row, placing sts. as for 2nd size on chart.
4th and 5th sizes: beg. with 2 rows A., then foll. chart from 21st row, placing sts. as for 3rd size on chart.
Keeping patt. correct as set and working extra sts. into patt. as they occur, inc. 1 st. at each end of 5th and every foll. 6th(6th:6th:12th:12th) row until there are 63(67:71:73:77) sts.
Cont. straight until sleeve measures 15(20:25:31:35) cm. (5¾(7¾:9¾:12¼:13¾) in.) from beg., ending with a p. row.
(Patt. at this point should correspond to patt. at armhole shaping of back and front).

Shape Sleeve Top
Cont. in patt. as set.
Cast off 4 sts. at beg. of next 2 rows.
Dec. 1 st. at each end of next and foll. 6(7:12:13:15) alt. rows, then dec. 1 st. at each end of next 5(6:3:3:1) rows. [31(31:31:31:35) sts.]
Cast off 3(3:3:3:4) sts. at beg. of next 6 rows.
Now cast off 4(4:4:4:3) sts. at beg. of foll. 2 rows.
Cast off rem. 5 sts.
Sew up right shoulder seam.

NECKBAND

With 2¾mm. needles and A, pick up and k. 82(88:96:100:108) sts., including sts. on holder.
Work in k.1, p.1 rib for 2 cm. (¾ in.)
Cast off loosely in rib.

LEFT SHOULDER EDGING

(1st and 2nd sizes only)

Sew up shoulder seam for 1 cm. (½ in.) at armhole edge.
With 2¾mm. needles and A, pick up and k.18(20) sts. from left back shoulder (including neckband), then 18(20) sts. from left front shoulder.
K.1 row.
Next row: k.20(22), cast off 2, k. next 10(12) sts., cast off 2, k. to end.
Next row: k. across row, casting on 2 sts. over cast off sts.
Cast off.

MAKING UP

Press all pieces except ribbing with a warm iron over a damp cloth.
Sew up left shoulder seam for 3rd, 4th and 5th sizes.
Set in sleeves.
Sew up side and sleeve seams.
Sew on buttons for 1st and 2nd sizes.
Press all seams.

Duck-pattern Shirt

1949

Long- or short-sleeved fitting shirt in stocking stitch with contrasting, embroidered duck design, ribbed collar and welts

★★ Suitable for knitters with some previous experience

MATERIALS

Yarn
Patons Clansman 4 ply
2(3:3) × 50g. balls Main Col. A
1(1:1) × 50g. ball Col. B
Oddments of yarn Col. C

Needles
1 pair 2¾mm.
1 pair 3¼mm.

Buttons
6 small

MEASUREMENTS

Chest
46(51:56) cm.
18(20:22) in.
6 months/1(1/2:2/3) approx. age

Length
30(33:38) cm.
11¾(13:15) in.

Short Sleeve Seam
7(9:10) cm.
2¾(3½:4) in.

Long Sleeve Seam
19(21:24) cm.
7½(8¼:9½) in.

TENSION

28 sts. and 36 rows = 10 cm. (4 in.) square over st. st. on 3¼mm. needles. If your tension square does not correspond to these measurements, adjust the needle size used.

ABBREVIATIONS

k. = knit; p. = purl; st(s). = stitch(es); inc. = increas(ing); dec. = decreas(ing); beg. = begin(ning); rem. = remain(ing); rep. = repeat; alt. = alternate; tog. = together; sl. = slip (transfer one stitch from left needle, knitwise unless otherwise stated, to right hand needle.); cont. = continue; patt. = pattern; foll. = following; folls. = follows; mm. = millimetres; cm. = centimetres; in. = inches; st. st. = stocking st.: one row k., one row p.; g. st. = garter st.: every row k.; incs. = increases; decs. = decreases; m.1 = make 1 st.: pick up horizontal loop lying before next st. and work into the back of it; y.fwd. = yarn forward; y.b. = yarn back.

NB Twist yarns on wrong side of work when changing col. to avoid a hole.

BACK

** Cast on 65(73:79) sts. with 2¾mm. needles and B.
K. 1 row.
Join in A, and work in border patt. as folls.:
1st row (right side): k.2B, * with A y.fwd., p.1, y.b., k.1B, rep. from * to last st., k.1B.
2nd row: k.1B, * p.1B, with A y.b., k.1, y.fwd., rep. from * to last 2 sts., p.1B, k.1B.
These 2 rows form patt.
Cont. in patt. until work measures 4(4:5) cm. (1½(1½:2) in.), ending with a 2nd row.
Break B.
Next row: with A, k.
Next row: p.5(6:7), m.1, * p.9(10:8), m.1, rep. from * to last 6(7:8) sts., p.6(7:8). [72(80:88) sts.]

Change to 3¼mm. needles and st. st.
Beg. with a k. row, work straight until back measures 20(23:25) cm. (7¾(9:9¾) in.) from beg., ending with a p. row.

Shape Armholes
Cast off 4 sts. at beg. of next 2 rows.
Now dec. 1 st. at each end of next and every alt. row until 52(56:60) sts. rem.
Work 1 row straight. **

Divide for Opening
Next row: k.24(26:28) sts., turn, leave rem. sts. on a spare needle.
Next row: cast on 4 sts., k.4, p. to end. [28(30:32) sts.]
Now, cont. in st. st., k.4 sts. at inside edge on every row, until back measures 30(33:38) cm. (11¾(13:15) in.) from beg., ending with a wrong side row.

Shape Shoulder
Cast off 4(5:4) sts. at beg. of next row.
Cast off 4(4:5) sts. at beg. of foll. 2 alt. rows.
Cast off rem. 16(17:18) sts.
With right side facing, rejoin yarn to rem. 28(30:32) sts., k. to end.
Next row: p. to last 4 sts., k.4.
Make 1st buttonhole in next row as folls.: k.2, y.fwd., k.2 tog., k. to end.
Complete to match 1st side with the addition of 5 more buttonholes, worked on every foll. 4th row.

FRONT

Work as for back from ** to **.
Cont. straight until front measures 27(30:34) cm. (10½(11¾:13¼) in.) from beg., ending with a wrong side row.

Divide for Neck
Next row: k.20(21:22) sts., turn, and leave rem. sts. on a spare needle.

Cont. on these 20(21:22) sts. for 1st side, dec. 1 st. at neck edge on every row until 12(13:14) sts. rem.
Work straight until front matches back armhole edge, ending with a wrong side row.
Now shape shoulder as for back.
With right side facing, rejoin yarn to rem. sts., cast off centre 12(14:16) sts., k. to end.
Complete to match first side.

SHORT SLEEVES

Cast on 45(49:53) sts. with 2¾mm. needles and B.
K. 1 row.
Beg. with a 1st row, work 4(4:5) cm. (1½(1½:2) in.) in border patt. as for back, ending with a 2nd row.
Break B.
Next row: with A, k.
Next row: with A, p.4, m.1, * p.9(10:11), m.1, rep. from * to last 5 sts., p.5. [50(54:58) sts.]
Change to 3¼mm. needles and, beg. with a k. row, work straight in st. st. until sleeve seam measures 7(9:10) cm. (2¾(3½:4) in.), ending with a p. row.

Shape Top
*** Cast off 4 sts. at beg. of next 2 rows.
Now dec. 1 st. at each end of next and every alt. row until 38 sts. rem.
Work 1 row straight.
Now dec. 1 st. at each end of every row until 14 sts. rem.
Cast off. ***

LONG SLEEVES

Cast on 39(43:47) sts. with 2¾mm. needles and B.
K. 1 row.

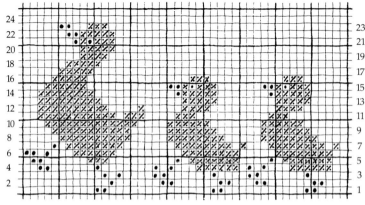

□ = Col A
🔲 = Col B
🔳 = Col C

Beg. with a 1st row, work 4(4:5) cm. (1½(1½:2) in.) in border patt, as for back, ending with a 2nd row.
Break B.
Next row: with A, k.
Next row: with A, p., inc. 1 st. at end of row. [40(44:48) sts.]
Change to 3¼mm. needles and, beg. with a k. row, work in st. st., shaping sides by inc. 1 st. at each end of 5th(1st:5th) and every foll. 10th(12th: 12th) row until there are 50(54:58) sts.
Cont. straight until sleeve seam measures 19(21:24) cm. (7½(8¼:9½) in.), ending with a p. row.

Shape Top

Work as for short sleeves from *** to ***.

COLLAR

Cast on 55(59:63) sts. with 2¾mm. needles and B.
K. 1 row.
Now, beg. with a 1st row, work 5(6:7) cm. (2(2¼:2¾) in.) in border patt. as for back.
Cast off.
Make another piece in the same way.

MAKING UP

Press work lightly on wrong side, taking care not to spoil patt.

Using chart, embroider 1 large and 4 small ducks across front of sweater, feet of ducks to come 2(3:4) cm. (¾(1¼:1½) in.) above end of border patt.
Work bodies in B.
Work eyes, legs and beaks in C.
Sew up shoulder, side and sleeve seams.
Set in sleeves.
Sew cast-off edge of each collar piece round neck, beg. at centre front and ending in centre of back opening border.
Sew cast-on edge of button border neatly behind buttonhole border.
Press all seams.
Sew on buttons.

Twin Set with Cabled Raglans   1954

Cardigan and jumper each worked in one piece from neck downwards, with cabled raglan sleeves, round necks and ribbed welts

★★★ Suitable for very experienced knitters only

MATERIALS

Yarn
Wendy Shetland 4 ply
Cardigan:
3(3:4:4) × 50g. balls
Sweater:
3(3:4:4) × 50g. balls

Needles
1 pair 3mm.
1 pair 3¼mm.
cable needle
1 circular 3¼mm., approx. 100 cm. (40 in. long)
st. holders

Buttons
Cardigan:
9(10:10:11)
Sweater:
5(5:6:7)

MEASUREMENTS

Chest
56(61:66:71) cm.
22(24:26:28) in.
2/3(4/5:6/7:8/9) approx. age.

Length
Cardigan:
39(43:43:47) cm.
15¼(16¾:16¾:18½) in.
Sweater:
38(42:42:46) cm.
15(16½:16½:18) in.

Sleeve Seam
Short Sleeve:
5(7:10:11) cm.
2(2¾:4:4½) in.

Long Sleeve:
26(29:32:36) cm.
10¼(11¼:12½:14) in.

TENSION

28 sts. and 36 rows = 10 cm. (4 in.) square over st. st. on 3¼mm. needles. If your tension square does not correspond to these measurements, adjust the needle size used.

ABBREVIATIONS

k. = knit; p. = purl; st(s). = stitch(es); inc. = increas(ing); dec. = decreas(ing); beg. = begin(ning); rem. = remain(ing); rep. = repeat; alt. = alternate; tog. = together; sl. = slip (transfer one stitch from left needle, knitwise unless otherwise stated, to right hand needle.); cont. = continue; patt. = pattern; foll. = following; folls. = follows; mm. = millimetres; cm. = centimetres; in. = inches; st. st. = stocking st.; one row k., one row p.; g. st. = garter st.; every row k.; incs. = increases; decs. = decreases; C4B = cable 4 back: sl. next 2 sts. onto cable needle and leave at back of work, k.2, then k.2 from cable needle; y.r.n. = yarn round needle; y.o.n. = yarn over needle.

NB The cardigan is worked in one piece, as is the sweater, beg. at the neck edge and working downwards.

CARDIGAN

Cast on 86(96:106:116) sts. with 3mm. needles.

Work 5 rows in k.1, p.1 rib.
Buttonhole row: rib 2, cast off 3, rib to end.
Next row: work in rib, casting on 3 sts. over those cast off.
Rib 1 row.
Change to 3¼mm. needles.
When necessary change to circular needle and cont. working in rows:
1st row: (k.1, p.1) 4 times, k.5(7:9:11), * y.r.n., p.1, k.4, p.1, y.o.n. *, k.10(12:14: 16), rep. from * to *, k.16(18:20:22), rep. from * to *, k.10(12:14:16), rep. from * to *, k.1, turn.
2nd row: sl.1, p. to last 12(14:16:18) sts., turn.
3rd row: sl.1, k.1, * y.r.n., p.1, k.4, p.1, y.o.n. *, k.12(14:16:18), rep. from * to *, k.18(20:22:24), rep. from * to *, k.12(14: 16:18), rep. from * to *, k.3, turn.
4th row: sl.1, p. to last 11(13:15:17) sts., turn.
5th row: sl.1, k.3, * y.r.n., p.1, C4B, p.1, y.o.n., * k.14(16:18:20), rep. from * to *, k.20(22:24:26), rep. from * to *, k.14(16: 18:20), rep. from * to *, k.5, turn.
6th row: sl.1, p. to last 10(12:14:16) sts., turn.
7th row: sl.1, k.5, * y.r.n., p.1, k.4, p.1, y.o.n. *, k.16(18:20:22), rep. from * to *, k.22(24:26:28), rep. from * to *, k.16(18: 20:22), rep. from * to *, k.7, turn.
8th row: sl.1, p. to last 9(11:13:15) sts., turn.
9th row: sl.1, k.7, * y.r.n., p.1, k.4, p.1, y.o.n. *, k.18(20:22:24), rep. from * to *, k.24(26:28:30), rep. from * to *, k.18(20: 22:24), rep. from * to *, k.9, turn.
10th row: sl.1, p. to last 8(10:12:14) sts., turn.
11th row: sl.1, k.9, * y.r.n., p.1, C4B, p.1,

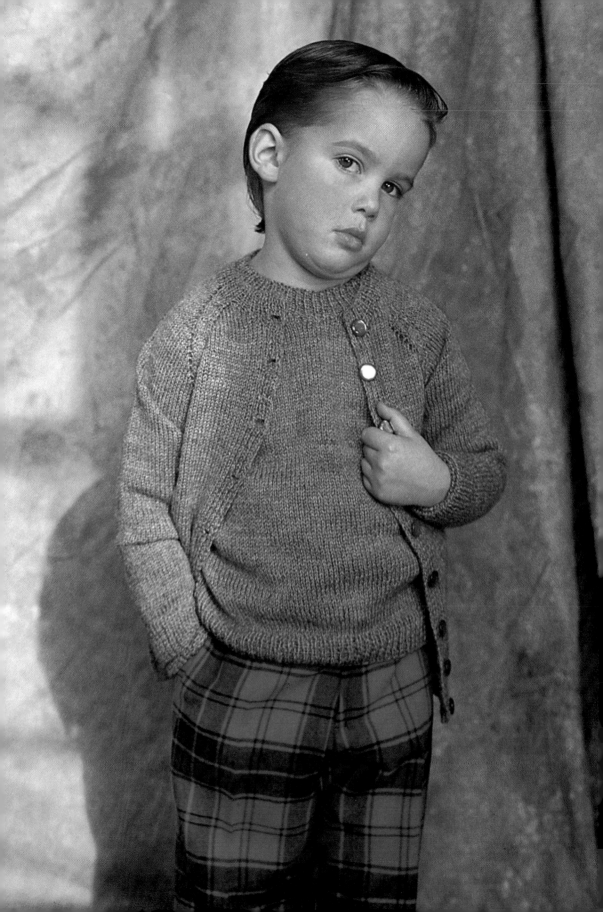

y.o.n. *, k.20(22:24:26), rep. from * to *, k.26(28:30:32), rep. from * to *, k.20(22:24:26), rep. from * to *, k.11(13:15:17), turn.

12th row: sl.1, p. to last 8 sts., k.1, turn.

13th row: sl.1, k.11(13:15:17), * y.r.n., p.1, k.4, p.1, y.o.n. *, k.22(24:26:28), rep. from * to *, k.28(30:32:34), rep. from * to *, k.22(24:26:28), rep. from * to *, k. to last 7 sts., (p.1, k.1) 3 times, p.1.

14th row: (k.1, p.1) 3 times, k.1, p. to last 8 sts., (k.1, p.1) 4 times.

Keep 8 sts. in k.1, p.1 rib at each end of rows throughout.

Cont. to work in this way, making sts. on each side of cable on every right side row, having 1 more st. in each front and 2 more in the back and sleeves each time, and working C4B every 6th row.

Work 7 more rows, ending with a k. row.

22nd row: work 2, cast off 3, work to end.

23rd row: working cables, work to cast off sts., cast on 3, work to end.

Work buttonholes in this way every 15th and 16th rows to end of work.

Cont. making 8 sts. on every right side row in the same way until there are 286(312:346:372) sts., ending with a right side row.

Divide for Sleeves

Next row: (k.1, p.1) 4 times, p.99(109:122:132), cast on 2, turn.

*** Foll. row:* k.68(74:82:88), cast on 2, turn.

Work sleeve on these 70(76:84:90) sts.

Work 3 rows.

Dec. 1 st. at both ends of next and every foll. 6th row until 50(52:54:56) sts. rem.

Cont. straight until sleeve measures 24(26:27:32) cm. (9½(10¼:10½:12½) in.), ending with a p. row.

Change to 3mm. needles.

Work 3(5:5:5) cm. (1¼(2:2:2) in.) in k.1, p.1 rib.

Cast off in rib.

Rejoin yarn to sts. on left needle.

Next row: p.138(150:166:178), cast on 2 sts., turn.

Now work second sleeve from **.

Rejoin yarn to sts. on left needle and p. to last 8 sts., rib 8.

Body

1st row: work 8 sts. in rib, k. across sts. of left front, cast on 4, k. across sts. of back, cast on 4, work across sts. of right front. [162(176:194:208) sts.]

Cont. straight until work measures 34(38:38:42) cm. (13¼(15:15:16½) in.) or 5 cm. (2 in.) shorter than required length, ending with a k. row.

Change to 3mm. needles.

Work 18 rows in k.1, p.1 rib, working the last buttonhole on the 15th and 16th of these rows.

Cast off loosely in rib.

MAKING UP

Press lightly, avoiding rib.

Sew up sleeve seams and join cast-on sts. at underarms.

Sew on buttons.

Press seams.

SWEATER

Cast on 35(39:43:47) sts. with 3¼mm. needles.

1st row: (k.1, p.1) 3 times, k.8(10:12:14), * y.r.n., p.1, k.4, p.1, y.o.n., *, k.8(10:12:14), rep. from * to *, k.1.

2nd and alt. rows: p. twice into first st., p. to last 6 sts., (k.1, p.1) 3 times.

3rd row: (k.1, p.1) 3 times, k.9(11:13:15), * y.r.n., p.1, k.4, p.1, y.o.n., *, k.10(12:14:16), rep. from * to *, k.3.

5th row: (k.1, p.1) 3 times, k.10(12:14:16), * y.r.n., p.1, C4B, p.1, y.o.n. *, k.12(14:16:18), rep. from * to *, k.5.

7th row: k.1, p.1, cast off 2, k.1, p.1, k.11(13:15:17), * y.r.n., p.1, k.4, p.1, y.o.n., * k.14(16:18:20), rep. from * to *, k.7.

NB On 8th row cast on 2 sts. over those cast off on 7th row.

9th row: (k.1, p.1) 3 times, k.12(14:16:18), * y.r.n., p.1, k.4, p.1, y.o.n., * k.16(18:20:22), rep. from * to *, k.9.

11th row: (k.1, p.1) 3 times, k.13(15:17:19), * y.r.n., p.1, C4B, p.1, y.o.n. *, k.18(20:22:24), rep. from * to *, k.11.

12th row: cast on 2, p. to last 6 sts., (k.1, p.1) 3 times.

13th row: (k.1, p.1) 3 times, k.14(16:18:20), * y.r.n., p.1, k.4, p.1, y.o.n. *, k.20(22:24:26), rep. from * to *, k.14.

14th row: as 12th.

15th row: (k.1, p.1) 3 times, k.15(17:19:21), * y.r.n., p.1, k.4, p.1, y.o.n. *, k.22(24:26:28), rep. from * to *, k.17.

Break yarn, leave sts. on holder.

Work left side of neck in same way, reading each row backwards to reverse shaping, omitting buttonhole and working y.r.n. in place of y.o.n., and y.o.n. in place of y.r.n.

Now join pieces as folls.:

16th row: (p.1, k.1) 3 times, p. to end, cast on 4(6:8:10), p. across sts. of first piece to last 6 sts., (k.1, p.1) 3 times. [156(166:176:186) sts.]

When necessary change to the circular needle and cont. working in rows.

17th row: k.1, p.1, cast off 2, k.1, p.1, k.16(18:20:22), * y.r.n., p.1, C4B, p.1, y.o.n. *, k.24(26:28:30), rep. from * to *, k.40(42:44:46), rep. from * to *, k.24(26:28:30), rep. from * to *, k. to last 6 sts., (p.1, k.1) 3 times.

NB On 18th row, cast on 2 sts. above cast-off sts. of 17th row.

Cont. in this way, making 8 sts. on every right side row, working cables on every 6th row and making 2(2:3:4) more buttonholes 8 rows apart until there are 284(310:344:370) sts., ending with a right side row.

Next row: cast off 6 sts. for underlap, p. until there are 97(107:120:130) sts. on needle, turn, cast on 2.

*** Foll. row:* k.64(70:78:84) sts., turn, cast on 2, sl. 35(39:44:48) sts. for back onto a holder.

Work sleeve on these 66(72:80:86) sts.

Short Sleeves

Work 4(6:8:10) rows straight.

Dec. 1 st. at both ends of next row and every 4th row until 60(64:68:72) sts. rem.

Change to 3mm. needles.

Work 6 rows in k.1, p.1 rib.

Cast off in rib.

Long Sleeves

Work 3 rows.

Dec. 1 st. at both ends of next and every foll. 6th row until 46(48:50:52) sts. rem.

Cont. straight until sleeve measures 23(26:29:33) cm. (9(10¼:11¼:13) in.), ending with a p. row.

Change to 3mm. needles.

Work 3 cm. (1¼ in.) in k.1, p.1 rib.

Cast off in rib.

Rejoin yarn to sts. on left needle, p.140(152:168:180) sts., turn and cast on 2.

Work second sleeve from **, leaving 78(84:92:98) sts. for front on second st. holder.

Rejoin yarn to rem. sts. of back, p. across these 41(45:50:54) sts., break yarn.

Sl. 35(39:44:48) sts. of other half of back onto same needle. [76(84:94:102) sts.]

Rejoin yarn at beg. of k. row.

*** Cast on 2 sts. at beg. of next 2 rows.

Work 20 rows straight.

Dec. 1 st. at both ends of next and foll. 20th row.

Cont. straight in st. st. until work measures 34(37:37:41) cm. (13¼(14½:14½:16) in.) or 4(5:5:5) cm. (1½(2:2:2) in.) shorter than required length, ending

with a p. row.
Change to 3mm. needles.
Work 12(18:18:18) rows in k.1, p.1 rib.
Cast off loosely in rib.
Rejoin yarn to sts. for front at beg. of a k. row.
Complete as for back from ***.

NECKBAND

With right side of work facing and 3mm. needles, pick up and k.76(86:96:106) sts. around neck edge.
Work 8 rows in k.1, p.1 rib, working the last buttonhole on the 3rd and 5th rows.
Cast off loosely in rib.

MAKING UP

Press work lightly avoiding rib.
Sew up side and sleeve seams.
Catch down base of underlap.
Sew on buttons.
Press seams.

Vest with Garter-stitch Yoke

Vest knitted in one piece starting with the front, in stocking stitch with garter yoke pattern and back opening

★ Suitable for beginners

NB Vest is photographed on baby worn with back ribbon fastening at front.

MATERIALS

Yarn
Phildar Perle 5
2 × 50g. balls

Needles
1 pair 2¾mm.
2½mm. crochet hook

Satin Ribbon
40 cm. approx.
15¾ in. approx.

MEASUREMENTS

Chest
41 cm.
16 in. (1/3 months old)

Length
22 cm.
8½ in.

TENSION

30 sts. and 40 rows = 10 cm. (4 in.) square over st. st. on 2¾mm. needles. If your tension square does not correspond to these measurements, adjust the needle size used.

ABBREVIATIONS

k. = knit; p. = purl; st(s). = stitch(es); inc. = increas(ing); dec. = decreas(ing); beg. = begin(ning); rem. = remain(ing); rep. = repeat; alt. = alternate; tog. = together; sl. = slip (transfer one stitch from left needle, knitwise unless otherwise stated, to right hand needle.); cont. = continue; patt. = pattern; foll. = following; folls. = follows; mm. = millimetres; cm. = centimetres; in. = inches; st. st. = stocking st.:

one row k., one row p.; g. st. = garter st.: every row k.; incs. = increases; decs. = decreases; ch. = chain ; d.c. = double crochet tr. = treble.

TO MAKE

Worked in one piece, beg. at lower edge of front.
Cast on 61 sts. with 2¾mm. needles.
K.13 rows.
Beg. with a k. row, work 37 rows in st. st., ending with a right side row.

Yoke
Next row: p.30, k.1, p.30.
Next row: k.
Next row: p.29, k.3, p.29.
Next row: k.
Next row: p.28, k.5, p.28.
Next row: k.
Cont. in st. st. with g. st. yoke patt. as set, taking 1 more st. on each side of yoke into g. st. on every wrong side row until there are 15 sts. in yoke patt., ending with a wrong side row.
Cont. working in yoke patt.:
Cast on 41 sts. at beg. of next 2 rows for sleeves. [143 sts.]
Now take the 8 sts. at each end of every

row into g. st. for cuff. AT THE SAME TIME when there are 21 sts. in g. st. for yoke work as folls.:
Next row (wrong side): k.8, p.42, k.43, p.42, k.8.
Next row: k.
Rep. last 2 rows 4 more times, then first of the rows again.

Shape Neck
Next row: work 69 sts., turn and leave rem. sts. on a spare needle.
Cast off 2 sts. at neck edge on next row.
Now dec. 1 st. at neck edge on the next 5 rows. [62 sts.]
Work 5 rows.
Inc. 1 st. at neck edge on next row.
Cast on 2 sts. at beg. of next row.
Work 1 row.
Cast on 13 sts. at beg. of next row. [78 sts.]
Cont. in g. st. and st. st. as set for 22 rows taking the centre back 28 sts. into g. st. for yoke, ending with a wrong side row.
Next row: cast off 41 sts., work to end.
Cont. straight on these 37 sts. for 50 rows, keeping 9 centre back sts. in g. st. and rem. in st. st.
Work 13 rows in g. st.
Cast off.
With right side facing rejoin yarn to rem. sts.
Cast off centre 5 sts. loosely and complete to match first side, reversing shapings.

MAKING UP

Press st. st. parts lightly on wrong side.
Work 1 row d.c. round neck, turn with 5 ch., work 1 tr. into the 3rd d.c. from end of last row, * work 2 ch., miss 2 d.c., work 1 tr. into next d.c., rep. from * to end.
Fasten off.
Sew up side and sleeve seams.
Join at centre back (or front as photographed) with satin ribbon.

Shoulder-buttoning Nautical Sweater 1955

Stocking stitch, striped sweater with set-in sleeves, ribbed yoke and welts, button fastening on both shoulders

★ Suitable for beginners

MATERIALS

Yarn
Sunbeam Pure New Wool 3 ply
2(3) × 25g. balls Main Col. A
2(2) × 25g. balls Col. B

Needles
1 pair 2¼mm.
1 pair double-pointed 3mm.

Buttons
6

MEASUREMENTS

Chest
46(51) cm.
18(20) in.
6 months/1(1/2) approx. age

Length
27(31) cm.
10½(12¼) in.

Sleeve Seam
17(20) cm.
6½(7¾) in.

TENSION

32 sts. and 44 rows = 10 cm. (4 in.) square over st. st. on 3mm. needles. If your tension square does not correspond to these measurements, adjust the needle size used.

ABBREVIATIONS

k. = knit; p. = purl; st(s). = stitch(es); inc. = increas(ing); dec. = decreas(ing); beg. = begin(ning); rem. = remain(ing); rep. = repeat; alt. = alternate; tog. = together; sl. = slip (transfer one stitch from left needle, knitwise unless otherwise stated, to right hand needle.); cont. = continue; patt. = pattern; foll. = following; folls. = follows; mm. = millimetres; cm. = centimetres; in. = inches; st. st. = stocking st.: one row k., one row p.; g. st. = garter st.: every row k.; incs. = increases; decs. = decreases; y.fwd. = yarn forward.

FRONT

Cast on 75(83) sts. with 2¼mm. needles and A.
1st row: k.1, * p.1, k.1, rep. from * to end.
2nd row: p.1, * k.1, p.1, rep. from * to end.
Rep. these 2 rows 5(6) more times, inc. 5 sts. evenly across last row. [80(88) sts.]
Change to double-pointed 3mm. needles and cont. in st. st. as folls.:
1st row: B, k. to end.
2nd row: B, p. to end.
3rd row: A, k. to end, return to beg. of row.
4th row: B, k. to end.
5th row: B, p. to end, return to beg. of row.
6th row: A, p. to end.
7th row: A, k. to end, return to beg. of row.
8th row: B, k. to end.
9th row: A, p. to end.
10th row: A, k. to end.
11th-20th rows: as 1st-10th rows, but reading k. for p. and p. for k. throughout. These 20 rows form the patt. and are rep. throughout.
Cont. in patt. until 58(70) rows have been worked in patt.

Shape Armholes

Keeping patt. correct, cast off 2 sts. at beg. of next 2 rows, then dec. one st. at each end of next and foll. 1(2) alt. rows. [72(78) sts.]
Cont. without shaping until 96(110) rows in all have been worked in patt., inc. one st. at end of last row. [73(79) sts.]
Change to 2¼mm. needles and A, and work 6 rows in rib as at beg.
Next row: rib 24(26), cast off 25(27) sts., rib to end.
Cont. on last 24(26) sts., rib 3(5) rows.
Next row: rib 2, (y.fwd., k.2 tog., rib 4) twice, y.fwd., k.2 tog., rib to end.
Rib 1 more row, then cast off in rib.
Rejoin yarn to the other 24(26) sts., and work to match, reversing buttonhole row.

BACK

Work as for front, omitting buttonholes.

SLEEVES

Cast on 41(45) sts. with 2¼mm. needles and A, work in rib as on front, inc. 11 sts. evenly across last row. [52(56) sts.]
Change to double-pointed 3mm. needles and cont. in patt. as on front, inc. 1 st. at each end of 15th and every foll. 16th(14th) row until there are 58(64) sts., then cont. without shaping until 58(70) rows in all have been worked in patt.

Shape Top
Keeping patt. correct, dec. 1 st. at each end of every row until 14(16) sts. rem. Cast off.

MAKING UP

Overlap front over back for 2 rows at shoulders and sew at armhole edges.
Set in sleeves.
Sew up side and sleeve seams.
Sew on buttons.
Press seams.

Satin-edged Lacy Shawl

Large, fine shawl with satin ribbon edging

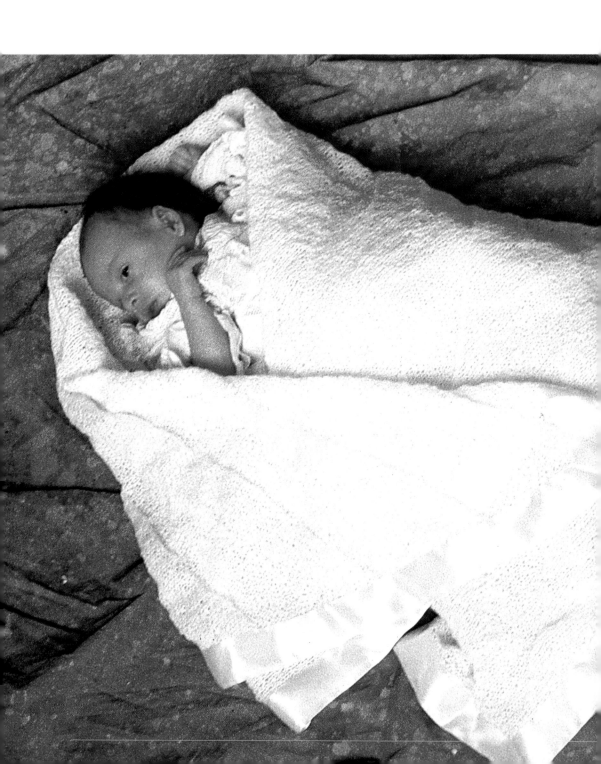

★★ Suitable for knitters with some previous experience

MATERIALS

Yarn
Sunbeam Pure New Wool 3 ply
17 × 25g. balls

Needles
1 pair 5mm. – extra long

Ribbon or blanket binding
5 metres

MEASUREMENTS

123 × 120 cm. approx.
48 × 47 in. approx.

TENSION

24 sts. and 28 rows = 10 cm. (4 in.) square

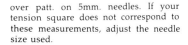

over patt. on 5mm. needles. If your tension square does not correspond to these measurements, adjust the needle size used.

ABBREVIATIONS

k. = knit; p. = purl; st(s). = stitch(es); inc. = increas(ing); dec. = decreas(ing); beg. = begin(ning); rem. = remain(ing); rep. = repeat; alt. = alternate; tog. = together; sl. = slip (transfer one stitch from left needle, knitwise unless otherwise stated, to right hand needle.); cont. = continue; patt. = pattern; foll. = following; folls. = follows; mm. = millimetres; cm. = centimetres; in. = inches; st. st. = stocking st.: one row k., one row p.; g. st. = garter st.: every row k.; incs. = increases; decs. = decreases.

TO MAKE

Cast on 288 sts.
1st row (right side): * k.12, p.12, rep. from * to end.
2nd row: as 1st.
3rd row: p.1, * k.12, p.12, rep. from * to last 23 sts., k.12, p.11.
4th and every alt. row: work across sts. as set.
5th row: p.2, * k.12, p.12, rep. from * to last 22 sts., k.12, p.10.
7th row: p.3, * k.12, p.12, rep. from * to last 21 sts., k.12, p.9.
9th row: p.4, * k.12, p.12, rep. from * to last 20 sts., k.12, p.8.
Cont. in this way, moving sts. over by one st. on every alt. row until work measures 120 cm. (47 in.) from beg., ending with a wrong side row.
Cast off loosely.

MAKING UP

Press.
Stitch on the binding all round edge of shawl, forming mitred corners.
Press edges.

Sweater with Circular-ribbed Yoke 1961

Simple, long-sleeved sweater in stocking stitch with stand-up collar, ribbed welts and circular-knitted yoke

★★ Suitable for knitters with some previous experience

MATERIALS

Yarn
Wendy Ascot DK
4(4:5:5) × 50g. balls.

Needles
1 pair 3¼mm.
1 pair 3¾mm.
1 set of 4 double-pointed 3¼mm.
1 set of 5 double-pointed 3¾mm.

MEASUREMENTS

Chest
51(56:61:66) cm.
20(22:24:26) in.
1/2(2/3:4/5:6/7) approx. age

Length
36(39:43:46) cm.
14(15¼:16¾:18) in.

Sleeve Seam
22(25:29:33) cm.
8½(9¾:11¼:13) in.

TENSION

24 sts. and 32 rows = 10 cm. (4 in.) square over st. st. on 3¾mm. needles. If your tension square does not correspond to these measurements, adjust the needle size used.

ABBREVIATIONS

k.=knit; p.=purl; st(s).=stitch(es); inc.= increas(ing); dec.=decreas(ing); beg.= begin(ning); rem. = remain(ing); rep. = repeat; alt. = alternate; tog. = together; sl. = slip (transfer one stitch from left needle, knitwise unless otherwise stated, to right hand needle.); cont. = continue; patt. = pattern; foll. = following; folls. = follows; mm. = millimetres; cm. = centimetres; in. = inches; st. st. = stocking st.: one row k., one row p.; g. st. = garter st.: every row k.; incs. = increases; decs. = decreases; p.s.s.o. = pass the sl. st. over.

BACK

Cast on 66(72:78:84) sts. with 3¼mm. needles.
Work 14(14:16:18) rows in k.1, p.1 rib.
Change to 3¾mm. needles and beg. with a k. row, work straight in st. st. until work measures 21(23:25:28) cm. (8¼(9: 9¾:11) in.) from cast-on edge, ending with a p. row.

Shape Armholes
Cast off 2(3:4:5) sts. at beg. of next 2 rows.
Work 2 rows straight.
Dec. 1 st. at both ends of next row and every foll. 3rd row until 54(56:58:60) sts. rem.
Work 2(1:2:1) rows straight, thus ending with a p. row.
Leave sts. on spare needle.

FRONT

Work as for back until 58(60:62:64) sts. rem. in armhole shaping, ending with a p.(k.:p.:k.) row.
2nd and 4th sizes only: p. 1 row.

Shape Neck
All sizes:
1st row: k.18, turn.
** Still dec. 1 st. at armhole edge on every 3rd row, cast off 6 sts. at neck edge on next and foll. alt. row.
Work 1 row straight.
Cast off 2 sts. at beg. of next row.
Work 1(0:1:0) row straight then cast off rem. sts.
Sl. centre 22(24:26:28) sts. onto holder and rejoin yarn to first of rem. 18 sts.
Work as for first side from ** to end.

SLEEVES

Cast on 36(38:40:42) sts. with 3¼mm. needles and work 14(14:16:18) rows in k.1, p.1 rib.
Change to 3¾mm. needles and beg. with a k. row, work 2 rows in st. st.
Cont. in st. st., inc. 1 st. at both ends of next and every foll. 6th row until there are 52(56:60:64) sts.
Cont. straight in st. st. until sleeve measures 22(25:29:33) cm. (8½(9¾:11¼: 13) in.).

Shape Top

Cast off 2(3:4:5) sts. at beg. of next 2 rows.
Work 2 rows straight, then dec. 1 st. at both ends of next and every foll. 3rd row until 40 sts. rem.
Work 2(1:2:1) rows straight.
Leave sts. on holder.

YOKE

Sew up all four armhole seams.
With right side facing and 3¾mm. double-pointed needles, k. up sts. around neck as folls.:
1st needle – 19 sts. down shaped edge of left front neck, 22(24:26:28) sts. from holder inc. 1 st. in centre, and 19 sts. up right side; 2nd needle – 40 sts. from sleeve inc. 1 st. in centre; 3rd needle – 54(56:58:60) from back, inc. 1 st. in centre; 4th needle – 40 sts. from left sleeve inc. 1 st. in centre. [198(202:206: 210) sts.]

Work 5 rounds in k.1, p.1 rib.
6th round: 1st needle – * sl. 1, k.2 tog., p.s.s.o., rib 17(17:17:19), k.3 tog. **, rib 15(17:19:17), rep. from * to **; 2nd needle – rib to end; 3rd needle – * sl. 1, k.2 tog., p.s.s.o., rib 15(15:15:17), k.3 tog. **, rib 13(15:17:15), rep. from * to **; 4th needle – rib to end.
Work 3 rounds in k.1, p.1 rib.
10th round: 1st needle – * sl.1, k.2 tog., p.s.s.o., rib 13(13:13:15), k.3 tog. **, rib 15(17:19:17), rep. from * to **; 2nd needle – rib 13, sl.1, k.2 tog., p.s.s.o., rib 9, k.3 tog., rib 13; 3rd needle – * sl.1, k.2 tog., p.s.s.o., rib 11(11:11:13), k.3 tog. **, rib 13(15:17:15), rep. from * to **; 4th needle – as 2nd.
Work 3 rounds in k.1, p.1 rib.
14th round: 1st needle – * sl. 1, k.2 tog., p.s.s.o., rib 9(9:9:11), k.3 tog. **, rib 15(17:19:17), rep. from * to **; 2nd needle – rib 11, sl. 1, k.2 tog., p.s.s.o., rib 9, k.3 tog., rib 11; 3rd needle – * sl. 1, k.2 tog., p.s.s.o., rib 7(7:7:9), k.3 tog. **, rib 13(15:17:15), rep. from * to **; 4th needle – as 2nd.
Work 3 rounds in k.1, p.1 rib.
18th round: 1st needle – * sl.1, k.2 tog., p.s.s.o., rib 5(5:5:7), k.3 tog. **, rib 15(17:19:17), rep. from * to **; 2nd needle – rib 9, sl. 1, k.2 tog., p.s.s.o., rib 9, k.3 tog., rib 9; 3rd needle – * sl. 1, k.2 tog., p.s.s.o., rib 3(3:3:5), k.3 tog. **. rib 13(15:17:15), rep. from * to **; 4th needle – as 2nd.
Work 3 rounds in k.1, p.1 rib.
22nd round: 1st needle – * sl. 1, k.2 tog., p.s.s.o., rib 5(5:5:7), k.3 tog. **, rib 7(9:11:9), rep. from * to **; 2nd needle – rib 7, sl.1, k.2 tog., p.s.s.o., rib 9, k.3 tog., rib 7; 3rd needle – * sl. 1, k.2 tog., p.s.s.o., rib 3(3:3:5), k.3 tog. **, rib 5(7:9:7), rep. from * to **; 4th needle – as 2nd.
Work 2 rounds in k.1, p.1 rib.
Change to double-pointed 3¼mm. needles.
Work 12 rounds in k.1, p.1 rib.

Cast off loosely in rib with 3¾mm. needle.

MAKING UP

Press.
Sew up side and sleeve seams.

Chunky, Moss-stitch Jacket

1942

Thick jacket with three-quarter-length set-in sleeves, rounded collar and narrow, knitted borders around whole garment

★★ Suitable for knitters with some previous experience

NB Sleeves are three-quarter length.

MATERIALS

Yarn
Phildar Wool DK
4(5:5) × 50g. balls

Needles
1 pair 3¼mm.
1 pair 4mm.

Buttons
5

MEASUREMENTS

Chest
56(61:66) cm.
22(24:26) in.
2/3(4/5:6/7) approx. age

Length
25(28:33) cm.
9¾(11:13) in.

Sleeve Seam
10(12:14) cm.
4(4¾:5½) in.

TENSION

21 sts. and 30 rows = 10 cm. (4 in.) square over patt. on 4mm. needles. If your tension square does not correspond to these measurements, adjust the needle size used.

ABBREVIATIONS

k.=knit; p.=purl; st(s).=stitch(es); inc.= increas(ing); dec.=decreas(ing); beg.= begin(ning); rem. = remain(ing); rep. = repeat; alt. = alternate; tog. = together; sl. = slip (transfer one stitch from left needle, knitwise unless otherwise stated, to right hand needle.); cont. = continue; patt. = pattern; foll. = following; folls. = follows; in. = inches; st. st. = stocking st.: one row k., one row p.; g. st. = garter st.: every row k.; incs. = increases; decs. = decreases.

RIGHT FRONT

Cast on 35(37:41) sts. with 3¼mm. needles.
K. 3 rows.

Change to 4mm. needles and work in patt. as folls.:
1st row (right side): k.1, * p.1, k.1, rep. from * to end.
2nd row: p.1, * k.1, p.1, rep. from * to end.
3rd row: p.1, * k.1, p.1, rep. from * to end.
4th row: k.1, * p.1, k.1, rep. from * to end.
These 4 rows form patt.
Work 4(0:0) more patt. rows.
1st buttonhole row: patt. 2 sts., cast off 2 sts., patt. to end.
2nd buttonhole row: patt., casting on 2 sts. over those cast off on previous row.
Patt. 8(12:14) rows.
Rep. 1st and 2nd buttonhole rows.
Cont. in this way until there are 3 buttonholes.
Work 7(9:13) rows straight after completion of 3rd buttonhole, thus ending with a right side row.

Shape Armhole
Keeping patt. correct, cont. to work buttonholes as before:
Cast off 3 sts. at beg. of next row.
Work 1 row.
Dec. 1 st. at armhole edge on next 3(5:5) rows.
Work 1 row.
Dec. 1 st. at beg. of next row. [28(28:32) sts.]
Work straight in patt. until 5 buttonholes have been worked, ending with 6(2:4) rows straight, and a wrong side row.

Shape Neck
Cast off 5 sts. at beg. of next row.
3rd size only: work 1 row, cast off 2 sts. at beg. of next and foll. alt. row.
All sizes: dec. 1 st. at neck edge on every row until 15(16:16) sts. rem.
Work straight in patt. until armhole measures 12(13:15) cm. (4¾(5:5¾) in.), ending at armhole edge.

Shape Shoulder
Cast off 5 sts. at beg. of next and foll. alt. row.
Work 1 row.
Cast off rem. 5(6:6) sts.

LEFT FRONT

Work to match right front, omitting buttonholes and reversing shapings.

BACK

Cast on 61(67:71) sts. with 3¼mm. needles.
K. 3 rows.
Change to 4mm. needles and work in patt. as for front until back matches front to beg. of armhole shaping, ending with a wrong side row.

Shape Armholes
Cast off 3 sts. at beg. of next 2 rows.
Dec. 1 st. at each end of next 3(5:5) rows.
Work 1 row.
Dec. 1 st. at each end of next row. [47(49:53) sts.]
Work straight in patt. until back matches front to beg. of shoulder shaping, ending with a wrong side row.

Shape Shoulders
Cast off 5 sts. at beg. of next 4 rows.
Cast off 5(6:6) sts. at beg. of next 2 rows.
Cast off rem. 17(17:21) sts.

SLEEVES

Cast on 35(39:43) sts. with 3¼mm. needles.
K. 3 rows.
Change to 4mm. needles and work in patt. as for front, AT THE SAME TIME inc. 1 st. at each end of every 3rd(4th:5th) row until there are 49(53:57) sts., taking inc. sts. into patt.
Work straight in patt. until sleeve measures 10(12:14) cm. (4(4¾:5½) in.), or required length, ending with a wrong side row.

Shape Top

Cast off 3 sts. at beg. of next 2 rows.
Dec. 1 st. at each end of next and every foll. alt. row until 21(25:25) sts. rem.
Dec. 1 st. at each end of every row until 11 sts. rem.
Cast off.

RIGHT FRONT BORDER

With right side facing and 3¼mm. needles, k. 48(54:60) sts. evenly up right front edge.
K. 2 rows.
Cast off.

LEFT FRONT BORDER

Work to match right front, but along left front edge.

COLLAR

Cast on 58(62:68) sts. with 3¼mm. needles.
K. 3 rows.
Change to 4mm. needles and work as folls.:
1st row (right side): k.
2nd row: k.3, p. to last 3 sts., k.3.
These 2 rows form patt.
Cont. straight in patt. as set until collar measures 4 cm. (1½ in.), ending with a 2nd row.

Shape Collar

Next row: k.7, k.2 tog., (k.12(13:15), k.2 tog.) 3 times, k.7(8:8). [54(58:64) sts.]
Work 3 rows.
Next row: k.7, k.2 tog., (k.11(12:14), k.2 tog.) 3 times, k.6(7:7). [50(54:60) sts.]
Work 1 row.
Next row: k.7, k.2 tog., (k.10(11:13), k.2 tog.) 3 times, k.5(6:6). [46(50:56) sts.]
Work 1 row.
Cast off.

MAKING UP

Sew up shoulder seams.
Sew cast-off edge of collar in position, allowing for front overlap.
Sew up side and sleeve seams.
Set in sleeves.
Sew on buttons.

Double-breasted Cotton Shirt 1938

Long-sleeved, collared shirt in stocking stitch, with ribbed yoke and double-breasted front opening

★ Suitable for beginners

MATERIALS

Yarn
Patons Cotton Top
5(5:6) × 50g. balls

Needles
1 pair 3¼mm.
1 pair 4mm.

Buttons
4

MEASUREMENTS

Chest
61(66:71) cm.
24(26:28) in.
4/5(6/7:8/9) approx. age

Length
42(46:49) cm.
16½(18:19¼) in.

Sleeve Seam
27(31:34) cm.
10½(12¼:13¼) in.

TENSION

20 sts. and 26 rows = 10 cm. (4 in.) square over st. st. on 4mm. needles. If your tension square does not correspond to these measurements, adjust the needle size used.

ABBREVIATIONS

k. = knit; p. = purl; st(s). = stitch(es); inc. = increas(ing); dec. = decrcas(ing); beg. = begin(ning); rem. = remain(ing); rep. = repeat; alt. = alternate; tog. = together;
sl. = slip (transfer one stitch from left needle, knitwise unless otherwise stated, to right hand needle.); cont. = continue; patt. = pattern; foll. = following; folls. = follows; mm. = millimetres; cm. = centimetres; in. = inches; st. st. = stocking st.: one row k., one row p.; g. st. = garter st.: every row k.; incs. = increases; decs. = decreases; m.1 = make 1 st.: pick up horizontal loop lying before next st. and k. into the back of it.

BACK

** Cast on 53(57:63) sts. with 3¼mm. needles.
1st row (right side): k.1, * p.1, k.1, rep. from * to end.
2nd row: p.1, * k.1, p.1, rep. from * to end.
Rep. last 2 rows until work measures 5 cm. (2 in.), ending with a 1st row.
Next row: rib 4(1:4) sts., m.1, * rib 5, m.1, rep. from * to last 4(1:4) sts., rib 4(1:4). [63(69:75) sts.]
Change to 4mm. needles and st. st.
Beg. with a k. row, work straight until back measures 28(31:33) cm. (11(12¼:13) in.) at centre from beg., ending with a wrong side row.

Shape Armholes

Cast off 3 sts. at beg. of next 2 rows.
Dec. 1 st. at each end of every row until 47(53:55) sts. rem.
2nd size only:
Now dec. 1 st. at each end of foll. alt. row. [47(51:55) sts.] **
All sizes:
With wrong side facing, and beg. with a 1st row, work in k.1, p.1 rib over all sts. until back measures 42(46:49) cm. (16½(18:19¼) in.) at centre from beg., ending with a wrong side row.

Shape Shoulders

Cast off 4(4:5) sts. at beg. of next 2 rows, then 4(5:5) sts. at beg. of next 4 rows.
Cast off rem. 23(23:25) sts.

FRONT

Work as for back from ** to **.
All sizes:
Work yoke as folls.:
Next row: k.1, rib 11(13:14), p.23(23:25) sts., rib 12(14:15).
Next row: rib 12(14:15), turn and leave rem. 35(37:40) sts., cont. on these 12(14:15) sts. for first side as folls.:
Next row: cast on 23(23:25) sts., (k.2, p.21(21:23) on cast-on sts.), rib to end.
Keeping 2 sts. at front edge in g. st., 21(21:23) sts. in st. st. and rem. in rib, work straight until front measures 37(41:44) cm. (14½(16:17¼) in.) at centre from beg., ending at front edge.

Shape Neck

Cast off 11(11:12) sts. at beg. of next row.

Cast off 3 sts. at beg. of foll. 3 alt. rows.
Now dec. 1 st. at neck edge on every row until 12(14:15) sts. rem.
Cont. until front matches back at armhole edge, ending with a wrong side row.

Shape Shoulder
Cast off 4(4:5) sts. at beg. of next row.
Cast off 4(5:5) sts. at beg. of foll. 2 alt. rows.
With right side facing, rejoin yarn to rem. 35(37:40) sts., k.23(23:25) sts., rib to end.
Complete to match first side, reversing all shapings and making 2 sets of buttonholes thus, 1st set to come 1 cm. (½ in.) above beg. of yoke, 2nd set to come 1 cm. (½ in.) below beg. of neck shaping:
1st buttonhole row (right side): k.2, cast off 3, k.13(13:15), cast off 3 sts., work to end.
2nd buttonhole row: work back, casting on 3 sts. over each set of those cast off.

SLEEVES

Cast on 31(33:35) sts. with 3¼mm. needles.

Work 5 cm. (2 in.) in k.1, p.1 rib as for back, ending with a 1st row.
Next row: rib 3(4:3), m.1, * rib 8(5:4), m.1, rep. from * to last 4(4:4) sts., rib 4(4:4). [35(39:43) sts.]
Change to 4mm. needles and, beg. with a k. row, work in st. st., shaping sides by inc. 1 st. at each end of 5th and every foll. 8th(10th:12th) row until there are 43(47:51) sts.
Work straight until sleeve seam measures 27(31:34) cm. (10½(12¼:13¼) in.), ending with a p. row.

Shape Top
Cast off 3 sts. at beg. of next 2 rows.
Now dec. 1 st. at each end of next and every alt. row until 19 sts. rem.
P. 1 row.
Now dec. 1 st. at each end of every row until 11 sts. rem.
Cast off.

COLLAR

Cast on 57(61:65) sts. with 3¼mm.

needles.
Work 5 rows in g. st.
Change to 4mm. needles.
Next row: k.
Next row: k.3, p. to last 3 sts., k.3.
Rep. last 2 rows 10(11:12) more times.

Shape Collar
Cast off 4 sts. at beg. of next 8 rows.
Cast off rem. 25(29:33) sts.

MAKING UP

Press lightly on wrong side, omitting ribbing on welt and cuffs, taking care not to spoil the rib yoke.
Sew up shoulder, side and sleeve seams.
Set in sleeves.
Catch down cast-on sts. of underlap on left side of yoke at back of work.
Pin cast-off edge of collar all round neck, beg. and ending at centre front, sew in position.
Press all seams.
Sew on buttons.

Russian Blouse

1933

High-necked Russian blouse in moss stitch with side-buttoning front, set-in sleeves and ribbed welts

★★ Suitable for knitters with some previous experience

MATERIALS

Yarn
Lister Lee Motoravia 4 ply
4 × 50g. balls

Needles
1 pair 3mm.
1 pair 3¼mm.

Buttons
6 small

MEASUREMENTS

Chest
71 cm.
28 in.
6/7 approx. age

Length
38 cm.
15 in.

Sleeve Seam
34 cm.
13¼ in.

TENSION

28 sts. and 32 rows = 10 cm. (4 in.) square over patt. on 3¼mm. needles. If your tension square does not correspond to these measurements, adjust the needle size used.

ABBREVIATIONS

k. = knit; p. = purl; st(s). = stitch(es); inc. = increas(ing); dec. = decreas(ing); beg. = begin(ning); rem. = remain(ing); rep. = repeat; alt. = alternate; tog. = together; sl. = slip (transfer one stitch from left needle, knitwise unless otherwise stated, to right hand needle.); cont. = continue; patt. = pattern; foll. = following; folls. = follows; mm. = millimetres; cm. = centimetres; in. = inches; st. st. = stocking st.: one row k., one row p.; g. st. = garter st.: every row k.; incs. = increases; decs. = decreases.

BACK

Cast on 100 sts. with 3mm. needles.
Work 10 rows in k.1, p.1 rib.
Change to 3¼mm. needles and patt. as folls.:
1st row (right side): * p.1, k.1, rep. from * to end.
2nd row: as 1st.
3rd row: * k.1, p.1, rep. from * to end.
4th row: as 3rd.
These 4 rows form patt.
Working in patt., cont. until back measures 23 cm. (9 in.), ending with a wrong side row.

Shape Armholes
Cast off 6 sts. at beg. of next 2 rows. **
Cont. straight until armholes measure 15 cm. (5¾ in.).

Shape Shoulders
Cast off 6 sts. at beg. of foll. 8 rows.
Cast off rem. sts. for back of neck.

FRONT

Work as for back to **.

Next row: work 24 sts., cast off 6 sts., work to end.

Cont. on 58 sts. for right front side of neck opening.

Work straight until armhole measures same as back to shoulder shaping, ending at side edge.

Shape Shoulder

Cast off 6 sts. at beg. of next and foll. 3 alt. rows.

Cast off rem. sts. for neck.

Return to rem. 24 sts. and work to match first side.

SLEEVES

Cast on 56 sts. with 3mm. needles.

Work 5 cm. (2 in.) in k.1, p.1 rib.

Change to 3¼mm. needles.

Work in patt. as for back, inc. 1 st. at each end of every 6th row until there are 68 sts.

Cont. straight until sleeve measures 34 cm. (13¼ in.).

Shape Top

Cast off 2 sts. at beg. of every row until 16 sts. rem.

Cast off.

LEFT FRONT BAND

Cast on 12 sts. with 3mm. needles.

Work in k.1, p.1 rib until band fits from bottom to top of left side of front opening.

Cast off.

Sew on band.

RIGHT FRONT BAND

Work as for left band, making 4 buttonholes thus, first on 8th and 9th rows, rem. 3 buttonholes at intervals of 10 rows:

1st buttonhole row: rib 5, cast off 2, rib to end.

2nd buttonhole row: rib 5, cast on 2, rib 5.

Cont. until right band matches left band.

Cast off.

Sew on band.

COLLAR

Sew up shoulder seams.

Cast on 20 sts. with 3mm. needles.

Work 4 rows in k.1, p.1 rib.

5th row: rib 4, cast off 2, rib 8 including st. left after casting off, cast off 2, rib to end.

Next row: rib 4, cast on 2, rib 8, cast on 2, rib to end.

Work in k.1, p.1 rib until collar fits around neck and overlaps for button opening.

Cast off.

MAKING UP

Press pieces with warm iron over damp cloth, omitting ribbing.

Set in sleeves.

Sew up side and sleeve seams.

Sew collar to neck.

Sew on buttons.

Press seams lightly.

Round-neck, Buttoned Playshirt 1948

Stocking stitch shirt with horizontal dash stitch panels, three-buttoned front placket and ribbed welts

★ Suitable for beginners

MATERIALS

Yarn
Phildar Perle 5
3(3:4:4) × 50g. balls

Needles
1 pair 2mm.
1 pair 2¾mm.
1 set of four double-pointed 2mm.

Buttons
4 small

MEASUREMENTS

Chest
51(56:61:66) cm.
20(22:24:26) in.
1/2(2/3:4/5:6/7) approx. age

Length
31(34:37:40) cm.
12¼(13¼:14½:15¾) in.

Sleeve Seam
23(25:29:31) cm.
9(9¾:11¼:12¼) in.

TENSION

30 sts. and 40 rows = 10 cm. (4 in.) square over st. st. with 2¾mm. needles. If your tension square does not correspond to these measurements, adjust the needle size used.

ABBREVIATIONS

k. = knit; p. = purl; st(s). = stitch(es); inc. = increas(ing); dec. = decreas(ing); beg. = begin(ning); rem. = remain(ing); rep. = repeat; alt. = alternate; tog. = together; sl. = slip (transfer one stitch from left needle, knitwise unless otherwise stated, to right hand needle.); cont. = continue; patt. = pattern; foll. = following; folls. = follows; mm. = millimetres; cm. = centimetres; in. = inches; st. st. = stocking st.: one row k., one row p.; g. st. = garter st.: every row k.; incs. = increases; decs. = decreases; m.1 = make 1 st.: pick up horizontal loop lying before next st. and work into back of it.

BACK

** Cast on 73(81:89:97) sts. with 2mm. needles and work in rib as folls.:
1st row (right side): k.1, * p.1, k.1, rep. from * to end.
2nd row: p.1, * k.1, p.1, rep. from * to end.
Rep. last two rows for 5 cm. (2 in.), ending with a 1st row.
Inc. row: rib 6(6:4:4), (m.1, rib 6(7:8:9)) 10 times, m.1, rib to end. [84(92:100:108) sts.]
Change to 2¾mm. needles and work in patt. as folls.:
1st row (right side): k.18(21:24:27), p.2, k.44(46:48:50), p.2, k.18(21:24:27).
2nd row: p.15(18:21:24), k.3, p.2, k.3, p.38(40:42:44), k.3, p.2, k.3, p.15(18:21:24).
These 2 rows form patt.
Work straight in patt. until back measures 20(22:24:26) cm. (7¾(8½:9½:10¼) in.), ending with a wrong side row.

Shape Armholes

Keeping patt. correct, cast off 4 sts. at beg. of next 2 rows.
Dec. 1 st. at each end of next 3(5:7:9) rows.
Work 1 row.
Dec. 1 st. at each end of next and 0(0:1:1) foll. alt. row. [68(72:74:78) sts.] **
Work straight in patt. until armholes measure 11(12:13:14) cm. (4¼(4¾:5:5½) in.), ending with a wrong side row.

Shape Shoulders

Cast off 5 sts. at beg. of next 6 rows.
Cast off 4 sts. at beg. of next 2 rows.
Cast off rem. 30(34:36:40) sts.

FRONT

Work as for back from ** to **.
Work 1 row, thus ending with a wrong side row.

Divide for Opening

Next row: k.10(11:11:12), p.2, k.26(27: 28:29), leave these sts. on a spare needle. With right side facing, cast on a further 8 sts. for button border and work as folls.:
Next row: k.3, p.2, k.21(22:23:24), p.2, k.10(11:11:12). [38(40:41:43) sts.]
Next row: p.7(8:8:9), k.3, p.2, k.3, p.15(16: 17:18), k.3, p.2, k.3.

Cont. working in patt. as set until front measures 4(4:5:5) cm. (1½(1½:2:2) in.) less than back to beg. of shoulder shaping, ending with a wrong side row.

Shape Neck
Next row: cast off 11 sts., patt. to end.
Dec. 1 st. at neck edge on next 6(8:8:11) rows.
Now dec. 1 st. on every foll. alt. row 2(2:3:2) times. [19 sts.]
Cont. straight in patt. until front matches back to shoulder shaping, ending with a right side row.

Shape Shoulder
Cast off 5 sts. at beg. of next and 2 foll. alt. rows.
Work 1 row.
Cast off rem. sts.
With wrong side facing, rejoin yarn to rem. sts., and work as folls.:
Next row: k.3, p.2, k.3, patt. to end. [38(40:41:43) sts.]
Cont. in patt. as set, working 3 button-holes, 1st to come 1 cm. (½ in.) from beg. of opening, last to come 2 rows from neck, rem. buttonhole midway between, making each buttonhole as folls.:
1st row (right side): patt. to last 6 sts., cast off 3 sts., patt. to end.
2nd row: patt. 3 sts., cast on 3 sts., patt. to end.
Complete to match first side, reversing shapings.

SLEEVES
Cast on 47(51:53:61) sts. with 2mm. needles and work in rib as for back, for 5 cm. (2 in.), ending with a 1st rib row.
Inc. row: rib 3(1:1:3), (m.1, rib 4(6:5:7)) 10(8:10:8) times, m.1, rib to end. [58(60: 64:70) sts.]
Change to 2¾mm. needles and, beg. with a k. row, work in st. st., shaping sides by inc. 1 st. at each end of every 18th(16th:20th:22nd) row 3(4:4:4) times, 3 sts. in from edge. [64(68:72:78) sts.]
Work straight until sleeve measures 23(25:29:31) cm. (9(9¾:11¼:12¼) in.), ending with a p. row.

Shape Top
Cast off 4 sts. at beg. of next 2 rows.
Dec. 1 st. at each end of next and every foll. alt. row until 34(34:34:42) sts. rem.
Dec. 1 st. at each end of every row until 20 sts. rem.
Cast off.

NECK BORDER
Sew up shoulder seams.
With right side facing and set of 2mm. needles, k. up 8 sts. from button border, 22(24:26:28) sts. up right side of neck to shoulder, 35:(39:43:47) sts. across back neck, 22(24:26:28) sts. down left side of neck, and 8 sts. from buttonhole border. [95(103:111:119) sts.]
Work forward and back in rows.

1st row (wrong side): p.2, * k.1, p.1, rep. from * to last st., p.1.
2nd row: k.2, * p.1, k.1, rep. from * to last st., k.1.
Rep. 1st row once more.
1st buttonhole row: rib to last 7 sts., cast off 3 sts., rib to end.
2nd buttonhole row: rib, casting on 3 sts. over those cast off on previous row.

Rib 3 rows.
Cast off evenly in rib.

MAKING UP
Sew up side and sleeve seams.
Set in sleeves.
Sew cast-on edge of button border neatly behind buttonhole border.
Sew on buttons.

Woven-stitch Knitted Shirt

Long-sleeved, woven-stitch sweater with collar, three-buttoned placket and ribbed welts

★ Suitable for beginners

MATERIALS

Yarn
Pingouin Corrida 3 4 ply
3(4:5) × 50g. balls

Needles
1 pair 2¾mm.
1 pair 3¼mm.

Buttons
3

MEASUREMENTS

Chest
51(56:61) cm.
20(22:24) in.
1/2(2/3:4/5) approx. age

Length
33(37:40) cm.
13(14½:15¾) in.

Sleeve Seam
21(23:27) cm.
8¼(9:10½) in.

TENSION

32 sts. and 44 rows = 10 cm. (4 in.) square over patt. on 3¼mm. needles. If your tension square does not correspond to these measurements, adjust the needle size used.

ABBREVIATIONS

k.=knit; p.=purl; st(s).=stitch(es); inc.= increas(ing); dec.=decreas(ing); beg.= begin(ning); rem. = remain(ing); rep. = repeat; alt. = alternate; tog. = together; sl. = slip (transfer one stitch from left needle, knitwise unless otherwise stated, to right hand needle.); cont. = continue; patt. = pattern; foll. = following; folls. = follows; mm. = millimetres; cm. = centimetres; in. = inches; st. st. = stocking st.: one row k., one row p.; g. st. = garter st.: every row k.; incs. − increases; decs. = decreases; y.fwd. = yarn forward; y.b. =

yarn back; m.1 = make 1 st.: pick up horizontal loop lying before next st. and work into back of it; sl.1p. = sl. 1 st. purlwise.

FRONT

** Cast on 78(86:94) sts. with 2¾mm. needles.
Work in rib as folls.:
1st row (right side): k.2, * p.2, k.2, rep. from * to end.
2nd row: p.2, * k.2, p.2, rep. from * to end.
Rep. these 2 rows until work measures 5 cm. (2 in.), ending with a 1st row.
Next row: rib 4(3:2), * m.1, rib 7(8:9), from * to last 4(3:2) sts., m.1, rib to end. [89(97:105) sts.]
Change to 3¼mm. needles and work in patt. as folls.:
1st row (right side): k.1, * y.fwd., sl.1p., y.b., k.1, rep. from * to end.
2nd row: p.
3rd row: k.2, * y.fwd., sl.1p., y.b., k.1, rep. from * to last st., k.1.
4th row: p.
These 4 rows form patt.
Cont. in patt. until front measures 23(26:27) cm. (9(10¼:10½) in.), ending with a wrong side row.

Shape Armholes

Keeping patt. straight, cast off 4 sts. at beg. of next 2 rows.
Dec. 1 st. at each end of next 5 rows.
Work 1 row.
Dec. 1 st. at each end of next and every alt. row until 63(71:77) sts. rem. **
Work 1(3:7) rows.

Divide for Front Opening

Next row: patt. 29(33:36), turn and leave rem. sts. on a spare needle.
Work on left side of front as folls.:
Next row: cast on 5 sts., p. across these sts., p. to end. [34(38:41) sts.]
Work 15 rows in patt., thus ending with a right side row.

Shape Neck

Cast off 6 sts. at beg. of next row.
Cast off 3 sts. at beg. of foll. alt. row.

Dec. 1 st. at neck edge on every row until 15(18:20) sts. rem.
Work 0(1:2) rows, thus ending with a wrong side row.

Shape Shoulder

Cast off 5(6:7) sts. at beg. of next and foll. alt. row.
Work 1 row.
Cast off rem. 5(6:6) sts.
Next row: with right side facing rejoin yarn to 34(38:41) sts. from spare needle, patt. to end.
Next row: p. to last st., k.1.

Make Buttonholes

Next row: patt. 2, cast off 2, patt. to end.
Next row: p. to last 2 sts., cast on 2, p.1, k.1.
Work 4 rows in patt., working k.1 at end of wrong side rows.
Rep. last 6 rows once more, then first 2 rows again.
Finish to match left side, reversing shapings.

BACK

Work as for front from ** to **
Work straight until back measures same as front to beg. of shoulder shaping, ending with a wrong side row.

Shape Shoulders

Cast off 5(6:7) sts. at beg. of next 4 rows.
Cast off 5(6:6) sts. at beg. of next 2 rows.
Cast off rem. 33(35:37) sts.

SLEEVES

Cast on 42(42:46) sts. with 2¾mm. needles and work 5 cm. (2 in.) in rib as given for front, ending with a 1st row.
Next row: rib 3(3:2), * m.1, rib 9(6:7), rep. from * to last 3(3:2) sts., m.1, rib to end. [47(49:53) sts.]
Change to 3¼mm. needles and work in patt. as given for front, shaping sides by inc. 1 st. at each end of 7th(3rd:9th) and every foll. 6th(8th:8th) row until there are 63(67:73) sts., taking inc. sts. into patt.
Work straight until sleeve seam measures 21(23:27) cm. (8¼(9:10½) in.), ending with a wrong side row.

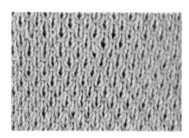

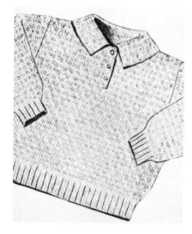

Shape Top

Keeping patt. straight, cast off 4 sts. at beg. of next 2 rows.

Dec. 1 st. at each end of next and every alt. row until 35(37:39) sts. rem.

Work 1 row.

Dec. 1 st. at each end of every row until 19(19:21) sts. rem.

Cast off.

COLLAR

Cast on 61(67:73) sts. with 3¼mm. needles and work in patt. as folls.:

1st row (right side): k.2, * y.fwd., sl.1p., y.b., k.1, rep. from * to last st., k.1.

2nd and every alt. row: k.2, p. to last 2 sts., k.2.

3rd row: k.2, m.1, * k.1, y.fwd., sl.1p., y.b., rep. from * to last 3 sts., k.1, m.1, k.2.

5th row: k.2, * k.1, y.fwd., sl.1p., y.b., rep. from * to last 3 sts., k.3.

7th row: k.2, m.1, * y.fwd., sl.1p., y.b., k.1, rep. from * to last 3 sts., y.fwd., sl.1p., y.b., m.1, k.2.

8th row: as 2nd.

Rep. these 8 rows once more, then 1st to 4th rows again. [71(77:83) sts.]

K.3 rows.

Cast off.

MAKING UP

Sew up shoulder, side and sleeve seams.

Set in sleeves.

Sew cast-on edge of collar to neck edge, beg. and ending at centre front.

Catch down underwrap at base of opening.

Sew on buttons.

Thick Cotton Sleeveless Pullover

Horizontal rib sleeveless pullover with ribbed lower welt, armholes and V-neck

1935

★ Suitable for beginners

MATERIALS

Yarn
Christian de Falbe Studio Yarns
Paradise Cotton
4(4:5:6) × 50g. balls.

Needles
1 pair 3mm.
1 pair 3¾mm.

MEASUREMENTS

Chest
61(66:71:76) cm.
24(26:28:30) in.
4/5(6/7:8/9:10/12) approx. age

Length
34(37:39:41) cm.
13¼(14½:15¼:16) in.

TENSION

23 sts. and 28 rows = 10 cm. (4 in.) square with double yarn over st. st. on 3¾mm. needles. If your tension square does not correspond to these measurements, adjust the needle size used.

ABBREVIATIONS

k. = knit; p. = purl; st(s). = stitch(es); inc. = increas(ing); dec. = decreas(ing); beg. = begin(ning); rem. = remain(ing); rep. = repeat; alt. = alternate; tog. = together; sl. = slip (transfer one stitch from left needle, knitwise unless otherwise stated, to right hand needle.); cont. = continue; patt. = pattern; foll. = following; folls. = follows; mm. = millimetres; cm. = centimetres; in. = inches; st. st. = stocking st.: one row k., one row p.; g. st. = garter st.: every row k.; incs. = increases; decs. = decreases; t.b.l. = through back of loops.

NB Use yarn double throughout.

BACK

Cast on 72(78:86:92) sts. with 3mm. needles.
Work 5(5:6:6) cm. (2(2:2¼:2¼) in.) in k.1, p.1 rib.
Change to 3¾mm. needles and patt. as folls.:
1st and 2nd rows: k.
3rd and 4th rows: p.
These 4 rows form patt.
Cont. in patt. until work measures 23(24:26:27) cm. (9(9½:10¼:10½) in.)

Cast off 5(6:6:6) sts. at beg. of next 2 rows.
Cast off 6(6:7:7) sts. at beg. of next 2 rows.
Cast off rem. 24(26:30:32) sts.

FRONT

Work as for back to **.

Shape Neck

Next row: patt. 26(28:32:33), work 2 tog., turn.
Working on 27(29:33:34) sts., cont. in patt., dec. at neck edge on alt. rows until 16(17:19:19) sts. rem.
Cont. without shaping until work measures same as back to shoulder shaping, ending at armhole edge.

Shape Shoulder

Cast off 5(5:6:6) sts., patt. to end.
Work 1 row.
Cast off 5(6:6:6) sts., patt. to end.
Work 1 row.
Cast off rem. 6(6:7:7) sts.
Rejoin yarn to rem. sts. at neck edge.
Next row: work 2 tog., patt. to end.
Work to match other side.

NECKBAND

Sew up right shoulder seam.

Shape Armholes

Cast off 2(2:3:3) sts. at beg. of next 2 rows.
Dec. 1 st. at each end of next 4 rows.
Dec. 1 st. at each end of next and foll. alt. rows until 56(60:68:70) sts. rem. **
Cont. without shaping until work measures 34(37:39:41) cm. (13¼(14½: 15¼:16) in.)

Shape Shoulders

Cast off 5(5:6:6) sts. at beg. of next 2 rows.

With 3mm. needles pick up and k. 40(42:42:44) sts. from left side front neck, 1 st. from centre front neck, 40(42:42:44) sts. from right front neck and 24(26:30:32) sts. from back neck. [105(111:115:121) sts.]
1st row: * k.1, p.1, rep. from * 30(32:34:36) times, k.2 tog.t.b.l., p.1, k.2 tog., * p.1, k.1, rep. from * 18(19:19:20) times.
2nd row: rib as set to within 2 sts. of centre front st., k.2 tog. t.b.l., k.1, k.2 tog., rib as set to end.
3rd row: rib to within 2 sts. of centre front st., k.2 tog. t.b.l., p.1, k.2 tog., rib to end.
Rep. 2nd and 3rd rows once, then 2nd row again.
Cast off loosely in rib.

ARMBANDS

Sew up left shoulder and neckband seam.
With 3mm. needles pick up and k.76(80:84:88) sts. evenly around armhole.
Work 6 rows in k.1, p.1 rib.
Cast off in rib.

MAKING UP

Sew up side and armband seams.

Polka-dot Jacket

1950

Round-neck jacket with contrasting polka-dot design, set-in sleeves, moss stitch welts and buttoned front border

★★ Suitable for knitters with some previous experience

MATERIALS

Yarn
Jaeger Luxury Spun 4 ply
2 × 50g. balls Main Col. A
1 × 50g. ball Col. B

Needles
1 pair 2¾mm.
1 pair 3¼mm.
safety pins

Buttons
6

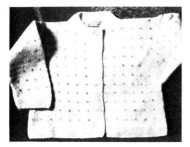

MEASUREMENTS

Chest
51 cm.
20 in. (1/2 approx. age)

Length
28 cm.
11 in.

Sleeve Seam
18 cm.
7 in.

TENSION

28 sts. and 36 rows = 10 cm. (4 in.) square over st. st. on 3¼mm. needles. If your tension square does not correspond to these measurements, adjust the needle size used.

ABBREVIATIONS

k.=knit; p.=purl; st(s).=stitch(es); inc.= increas(ing); dec.=decreas(ing); beg.= begin(ning); rem. = remain(ing); rep. = repeat; alt. = alternate; tog. = together; sl. = slip (transfer one stitch from left needle, knitwise unless otherwise stated, to right hand needle.); cont. = continue;

patt. = pattern; foll. = following; folls. = follows; mm. = millimetres; cm. = centimetres; in. = inches; st. st. = stocking st.: one row k., one row p.; g. st. = garter st.: every row k.; incs. = increases; decs. = decreases.

N.B. When working 2 col. patt., strand yarns loosely

BACK

Cast on 77 sts. with 2¾mm. needles and A.
Work in border patt. as folls.:
1st row: k.1, * p.1, k.1, rep. from * to end.
Rep. this row 9 times more, inc. 1 st. at each end of last row. [79 sts.]
Change to 3¼mm. needles and work in patt. as folls.:
1st row (right side): with A, k.
2nd row: with A, p.
Join in B.
3rd row: k.4 A, 1B, * 6A, 1B, rep. from * to last 4 sts., 4A.
4th row: with A, p.
5th row: with A, k.
6th-11th rows: as 4th and 5th rows 3 times.
12th row: p. 4A, 1B, * 6A, 1B, rep. from * to last 4 sts., 4A.

13th-18th rows: as 1st and 2nd rows 3 times.

These 18 rows form patt.

N.B. Carry col. B loosely up side of work. Cont. straight in patt. until back measures 18 cm. (7 in.) at centre from beg., ending with right side facing.

Shape Armholes

Cast off 4 sts. at beg. of next 2 rows, working in patt. throughout.

Dec. 1 st. at each end of next and every alt. row until 57 sts. rem.

Cont. straight until back measures 28 cm. (11 in.) at centre from beg., ending with right side facing.

Shape Shoulders

Cast off 5 sts. at beg. of next 6 rows.

Leave rem. 27 sts. on a spare needle.

LEFT FRONT

Cast on 41 sts. with 2¾mm. needles and A.

Work 10 rows border patt. as for back, but inc. 1 st. at end of last row. [42 sts.]

Change to 3¼mm. needles and, beg. with 1st row, work in patt. as for back, working 6 sts. at front edge in border patt. as folls.:

1st row (right side): with A, k. to last 6 sts., (p.1, k.1) 3 times.

2nd row: (k.1, p.1) 3 times, p. to end.

Join in B.

3rd row: k. 4A, 1B, * 6A, 1B, rep. from * to last 9 sts., 3A, (p.1, k.1) 3 times with A.

Cont. in patt. thus until front measures same as back at side edge, ending with right side facing.

Shape Armhole

Cast off 4 sts. at beg. of next row.

Work 1 row straight, then dec. 1 st. at beg. of next and every alt. row until 32 sts. rem.

Keeping patt. correct, work straight until front measures 24 cm. (9½ in.) at centre from beg., ending with wrong side facing.

Shape Neck

Next row: (k.1, p.1) 3 times, sl. these 6 sts. onto a safety pin for neck border, cast off 3 sts., patt. to end.

Now dec. 1 st. at neck edge on every row until 15 sts. rem.

Work straight until front matches back at armhole edge, ending with right side facing.

Shape Shoulder

Cast off 5 sts. at beg. of next and foll. 2 alt. rows.

RIGHT FRONT

Work to match left front, but make 5 buttonholes, 1st to come 2 cm. (¾ in.) above lower edge, 5th, 4 cm. (1½ in.) below beg. of neck shaping and rem. 3 spaced evenly between.

Mark position of buttons on left border with pins to ensure even spacing, then work holes to correspond.

Make buttonhole:

1st row (right side): patt. 2, cast off 2, patt. to end.

2nd row: work back, casting on 2 sts. over those cast off.

Shape Neck

Work to match left front, but 1st row will read:

Break yarn, sl. first 6 sts. on a safety pin for neck border, rejoin yarn to rem. sts., cast off 3, patt. to end.

SLEEVES

Cast on 43 sts. with 2¾mm. needles and A.

Work 10 rows in border patt. as for back, but inc. 1 st. at end of last row. [44 sts.]

Change to 3¼mm. needles and beg. with 1st row, work in patt. as for back, shaping sides by inc. 1 st. at each end of 5th and every foll. 6th row until there are 58 sts., taking inc. sts. into patt.

Work straight until sleeve seam measures 18 cm. (7 in.), ending with same row of patt. as on back and fronts before start of armhole shaping.

Shape Top

Cast off 4 sts. at beg. of next 2 rows, then dec. 1 st. at each end of next and every alt.

row until 32 sts. rem.

Work 1 row straight.

Dec. 1 st. at each end of every row until 16 sts. rem.

Cast off.

NECK BORDER

Sew up shoulder seams.

With right side facing, using 2¾mm. needles and A, patt. 6 sts. from safety pin on right border, pick up and k.17 sts. up right side of neck, k.27 from back, pick up and k.17 down left side, then patt. 6 sts. from safety pin on left border. [73 sts.]

Work 3 rows in border patt.

Make a buttonhole in next 2 rows, then work a further 4 rows border patt.

Cast off in patt.

MAKING UP

Press lightly on wrong side, omitting borders.

Sew up side and sleeve seams, matching patt.

Set in sleeves.

Press all seams.

Sew on buttons.

Sweater with Cabled Cross-stitch 1949

Round-neck sweater in stocking stitch with cable crosses on yoke and cuff, with set-in sleeves and shoulder buttoning

★★ Suitable for knitters with some previous experience

MATERIALS

Yarn
Wendy Ascot 4 ply
3(4:4) × 50g. balls

Needles
1 pair 3mm.
1 pair 3¼mm.
1 cable needle
1 crochet hook
st. holder

Buttons
3

MEASUREMENTS

Chest
56(61:66) cm.
22(24:26) in.
2/3(4/5:6/7) approx. age

Length
36(39:42) cm.
14(15¼:16½) in.

Sleeve Seam
23(26:29) cm.
9(10¼:11¼) in.

TENSION

28 sts. and 36 rows = 10 cm. (4 in.) square over st. st. on 3¼mm. needles. If your tension square does not correspond to these measurements, adjust the needle size used.

ABBREVIATIONS

k. = knit; p. = purl; st(s). = stitch(es); inc. = increas(ing); dec. = decreas(ing); beg. = begin(ning); rem. = remain(ing); rep. = repeat; alt. = alternate; tog. = together; sl. = slip (transfer one stitch from left needle, knitwise unless otherwise stated, to right hand needle.); cont. = continue; patt. = pattern; foll. = following; folls. = follows; mm. = millimetres; cm. = centimetres; in. = inches; st. st. = stocking st.: one row k., one row p.; g. st. = garter st.: every row k.; incs. = increases; decs. = decreases; C4 = cable 4: sl. the next 2 sts. onto cable needle and hold at back of work, k.2 sts., k. sts. from cable needle.

BACK

Cast on 77(82:87) sts. with 3mm. needles.
1st row (right side): p.2, * k.3, p.2, rep. from * to end.
2nd row: k.2, * p.3, k.2, rep. from * to end.
Rep. these 2 rows for 4 cm. (1½ in.), ending with a right side row.
Inc. 7(10:13) sts. evenly across next row. [84(92:100) sts.]
Change to 3¼mm. needles.
Beg. with a k. row, work 10 rows in st. st.
Cable row: k.18(20:22), * C4, k.18(20:22), rep. from * twice.
St. st. 11(13:15) rows.
Cable row: k.7(8:9), * C4, k.18(20:22), rep. from * twice, C4, k.7(8:9).
St. st. 11(13:15) rows.
Rep. the last 24(28:32) rows once.
Cable row: k.18(22:26), (C4) 12 times, k.18(22:26).
St. st. 7 rows.

Shape Armholes

Cast off 4(5:6) sts. at beg. of next 2 rows. [76(82:88) sts.]
Dec. 1 st. at both ends of next 4 right side rows working (C4) 12 times across centre 48 sts. on the first of these rows. [68(74:80) sts.]
Work 3 rows straight.

Next row: k.10(13:16), (C4) 12 times, k.10(13:16).
Work 9 rows straight.
Cable row: k.2(1:4), (C4) 16(18:18) times, k.2(1:4).
St. st. 9 rows.
Cont. in patt. as set on the last 10 rows until armholes measure 13(14:14) cm. (5(5½:5½) in.), ending with a wrong side row.

Shape Shoulders

Cast off 6(7:8) sts. at beg. of each of next 4 rows and 7 sts. at beg. of foll. 2 rows.
Leave rem. 30(32:34) sts. on a spare needle, until needed for neckband.

FRONT

Work as for back until front measures 6 rows less than back to beg. of shoulder shaping, ending with a wrong side row. [68(74:80) sts.]

Shape Neck

Next row: patt. 24(26:28), turn and work on these sts. leaving rem. 44(48:52) sts. on a spare needle.
Dec. 1 st. at neck edge on next 5 rows. [19(21:23) sts.]

Shape Shoulder

Cast off 6(7:8) sts. at beg. of next row and foll. alt. row.
Work 1 row straight.
Cast off rem. 7 sts.
Next row: with right side of work facing sl. centre 20(22:24) sts. onto holder and rejoin yarn to first of rem. 24(26:28) sts., patt. to end.
Complete to match first side.

SLEEVES

Cast on 52(56:60) sts. with 3mm. needles.
1st row: k.
2nd row: p.
Cable row: k.2, (C4) 12(13:14) times, k.2.
St. st. 9 rows then rep. cable row.
P. 1 row.
Change to 3¼mm. needles.
Inc. row: k.1(3:5), * inc., k.6, rep. from * 6 times, inc., k.1(3:5). [60(64:68) sts.]
Beg. with a p. row, work straight in st. st. until sleeve measures 23(26:29) cm. (9(10¼:11¼) in.), ending with a p. row.

Shape Top

Cast off 4(5:6) sts. at beg. of next 2 rows

Now dec. 1 st. at both ends of every right side row until 32 sts. rem. on all sizes.
P. 1 row.
Dec. 1 st. at both ends of next 8 rows.
Cast off rem. 16 sts.

NECKBAND

Sew up right shoulder seam.
With right side of work facing and 3mm. needles, pick up and k. 17 sts. down left front neck, k. across 20(22:24) sts. at centre front, pick up and k. 17 sts. up right front neck then k. across 30(32:34) sts. of back neck. [84(88:92) sts.]
P. 1 row.
Cable row: (C4) 21(22:23) times.
Work 5 rows in p.2, k.2 rib then rep. cable row.
P. 1 row.
Cast off.

MAKING UP

Sew up left shoulder seam for 3 cm. (1¼ in.) from armhole edge.
Set in sleeves.
Sew up side and sleeve seams.
Work 1 row of double crochet (see page 162) across left back shoulder.
Work 1 row of double crochet across left front shoulder making 3 button loops.
Sew 3 buttons to back shoulder to correspond with button loops.

Raised Pattern Sweater

1960

Short- or long-sleeved sweater with raised pattern bands, raglan sleeves and ribbed welts

★ Suitable for beginners

MATERIALS

Yarn
Yarnworks Cotton
Short Sleeved Version:
3(4:4:5) × 50g. balls
Long Sleeved Version:
4(5:5:6) × 50g. balls

Needles
1 pair 3¼mm.
1 pair 4mm.

MEASUREMENTS

Chest
46(51:56:61) cm.
18(20:22:24) in.
6 months/1(1/2:2/3:4/5) approx. age

Length
27(30:34:38) cm.
10½(11¾:13¼:15) in.

Sleeve Seam

Short version:
5(5:5:5) cm.
2(2:2:2) in.

Long version:
19(22:24:27) cm.
7½(8½:9½:10½) in.

TENSION

20 sts. and 30 rows = 10 cm. (4 in.) square over patt. on 4mm. needles. If your tension square does not correspond to these measurements, adjust the needle size used.

ABBREVIATIONS

k. = knit; p. = purl; st(s). = stitch(es); inc. = increas(ing); dec. = decreas(ing); beg. = begin(ning); rem. = remain(ing); rep. = repeat; alt. = alternate; tog. = together; sl. = slip (transfer one stitch from left needle, knitwise unless otherwise stated, to right hand needle.); cont. = continue; patt. = pattern; foll. = following; folls. = follows; mm. = millimetres; cm. = centimetres; in. = inches; st. st. = stocking st.: one row k., one row p.; g. st. = garter st.: every row k.; incs. = increases; decs. = decreases; t.b.l. = through back of loops.

BACK

Cast on 49(55:59:65) sts. with 3¼mm. needles.
1st row (right side): k.1 t.b.l., * p.1 t.b.l., k.1 t.b.l., rep. from * to end.
2nd row: p.1 t.b.l., * k.1 t.b.l., p.1 t.b.l., rep. from * to end.
These 2 rows form rib, rep. for 4 cm. (1½ in.), ending with a wrong side row.
Change to 4mm. needles, beg. patt. as folls.:
1st row (right side): k.
2nd row: p.
3rd row: k.
4th row: k. t.b.l.
5th row: k.
6th row: p.1, * k.1, p.1, rep. from * to end.
7th row: k.
8th row: k.1, * p.1, k.1, rep. from * to end.
9th row: k.
10th row: k. t.b.l.
These 10 rows form patt.
Work in patt. until back measures 16(19: 22:24) cm. (6¼(7½:8½:9½) in.) from beg., ending with a wrong side row.

Shape Raglan
Cast off 3 sts. at beg. of next 2 rows.
Dec. 1 st. at each end of next row then every foll. 4th row 5(2:2:2) times more. [31(43:47:53) sts.]
Dec. 1 st. at each end of every foll. alt. row 5(11:12:15) times. [21(21:23:23) sts.]
Work 1 row.
Break yarn, leave these sts. on holder.

FRONT

Work as for back.

SLEEVES

Short version only:
Cast on 41(43:43:45) sts. with 3¼mm. needles.
Work 4 rows in rib as for back.
Change to 4mm. needles.

Work in patt. as for back until sleeve measures 5 cm. (2 in.) from beg., ending with same patt. row as back to armhole.

Shape Raglan
Cast off 3 sts. at beg. of next 2 rows.
Dec. 1 st. at each end of next and every foll. 4th row 4(3:4:6) more times. [25(29:27:25) sts.]
Dec. 1 st. at each end of every foll. alt. row 5(7:6:5) times. [15 sts.]

Shape Neck
Next row: patt. 7, cast off 1 st., patt. to end.
Next row: patt. 7, join in a 2nd ball of yarn, and patt. rem. 7 sts.
Working both sides at same time with separate balls of yarn, and, keeping raglan edge straight, dec. 1 st. at neck edge on next 4 rows [3 sts. at each side of neck].
Cast off.

Long version only:
Cast on 29(31:33:35) sts. with 3¼mm. needles.
Work 4 cm. (1½ in.) in rib as for back, ending with a wrong side row.
Change to 4mm. needles and work in patt as for back AT THE SAME TIME inc. 1 st. at each end of 3rd and every foll. 6th(6th:10th:10th) row 5(5:4:4) more times. [41(43:43:45) sts.]
Cont. straight in patt. until sleeve measures 19(22:24:27) cm. (7½(8½:9½: 10½) in.) from beg., ending with same patt. row as back to armhole.

Shape Raglan and Neck
Work as for short version of sleeve.

NECKBANDS
Back Neckband
With 3¼mm. needles, pick up and k. 11 sts. from half of sleeve top, k.21(21:23:23) sts. from back neck, pick up and k. 11 sts. from half of other sleeve top. [43(43:45:45) sts.]
Beg. with a 2nd rib row, work 5 rows in rib.
Cast off in rib.

Front Neckband
Work as for back neckband.

MAKING UP
Sew up side and sleeve seams.
Sew up raglans.
Overlap neckbands at shoulders and sew straight edges along shaped edges of shoulders.

Ridged Stocking Stitch Sweater

Hemmed, ridge-pattern sweater with raglan sleeves, ribbed welts and back placket buttoning

★ Suitable for beginners

MATERIALS

Yarn
Georges Picaud Coton Canelle
3 × 50g. balls

Needles
1 pair 2¼mm.
1 pair 2¾mm.
st. holder.

Buttons
4 small

MEASUREMENTS

Chest
48 cm.
18¾ in. (6/9 months approx. age)

Length
21 cm.
8¼ in.

Sleeve Seam
15 cm.
5¾ in.

TENSION

33 sts. and 51 rows = 10 cm. (4 in.) square over patt. on 2¾mm. needles. If your tension square does not correspond to these measurements, adjust the needle size used.

ABBREVIATIONS

k. = knit; p. = purl; st(s). = stitch(es); inc. = increas(ing); dec. = decreas(ing); beg. = begin(ning); rem. = remain(ing); rep. = repeat; alt. = alternate; tog. = together; sl. = slip (transfer one stitch from left needle, knitwise unless otherwise stated, to right hand needle.); cont. = continue; patt. = pattern; foll. = following; folls. = follows; mm. = millimetres; cm. = centimetres; in. = inches; st. st. = stocking st.: one row k., one row p.; g. st. = garter st.: every row k.; incs. = increases; decs. = decreases; p.s.s.o. = pass the sl. st. over; y.r.n. = yarn round needle.

FRONT

Cast on 88 sts. with 2¼mm. needles.

Work 5 rows in k.1, p.1 rib.
Change to 2¾mm. needles.
Work 9 rows in st. st., beg. with a p. row.
10th row (right side): p.
These 10 rows form ridge patt., worked throughout.
Cont. in ridge patt. until a total of 63 rows have been worked from top of rib.

Shape Raglan

Cast off 5 sts. at beg. of next 2 rows.
Next row: sl.1, k.1, p.s.s.o., patt. to last 2 sts., patt. 2 tog.
Next row: p.
Rep. the last 2 rows until 48 sts. rem., ending with a p. row.

Shape Neck

Next row: sl.1, k.1, p.s.s.o., k.16, and leave these 17 sts. on a spare needle, k. next 12 sts. then leave these 12 sts. on holder, k. to last 2 sts., k.2 tog.
Work each side separately.
1st, 3rd, 5th and 7th rows: p.
2nd row: cast off 4 sts., k. to last 2 sts., k.2 tog.
4th row: cast off 4 sts., p. to last 2 sts., p.2 tog.
6th row: cast off 2 sts., k. to last 2 sts., k.2 tog.
8th row: k.2 tog. twice.
9th row: p.2 tog., break yarn and fasten off.
Rejoin yarn to neck edge of other side and work as for first side, reversing all shapings.

BACK

Work as for front until there are 62 sts., ending with 8th ridge.

Work Back Opening

Next row (wrong side): p. 33 sts., turn, leave rem. sts. on spare needle.
1st row: p.4, k. to last 2 sts., k.2 tog.
2nd row: p.
Rep. last 2 rows 3 times.
9th row: p.2, y.r.n., p.2 tog., p. to last 2 sts., p.2 tog.
Cont. working 2nd and 1st rows, making another buttonhole on 17th row, keeping to ridge patt., until 21 sts. rem.
Work 1 row, thus ending at neck edge, do not break yarn.
Leave sts. on a spare needle.
Join separate yarn to inner edge of rem. sts.
Work 2nd side as folls.:
Cast on 4 sts., p. to end.
1st row: sl.1, k.1, p.s.s.o., k. to last 4 sts., p.4.
2nd row: p.
Keeping to ridge patt., cont. working 1st and 2nd rows until 21 sts. rem.
Work 1 row.
Break yarn and leave sts. on spare needle.

SLEEVES

Cast on 48 sts. with 2¼mm. needles.
Work 5 rows in k.1, p.1 rib.
Change to 2¾mm. needles and work in ridge patt. as for front.
Inc. 1 st. at each end of every 6th row until there are 72 sts. and 73 rows have

been worked.

Shape Top

Cast off 5 sts. at beg. of next 2 rows.
Dec. 1 st. at each end of next and every alt. row until 26 sts. rem.
Now dec. 1 st. at each end of every row until 16 sts. rem.
Leave on spare needle.

NECKBAND

With 2¼mm. needles, work from left side of back, using yarn still attached as folls.:
1st row: across sts. of left back work p.2, y.r.n., p.2 tog., k.15, k.2 tog., across sts. of left sleeve work k.2 tog., k.12, k.2 tog., pick up and k. 14 sts. down left front neck, k. across 12 sts. at centre front, pick up and k. 14 sts. up right front neck, work across right sleeve as for left sleeve then, across sts. of right back, work k.17, p.4. [109 sts.]
2nd row: p.4, * p.1, k.1, rep. from * to last 5 sts., p.5.
3rd row: p.4, rib to last 4 sts., p.4.
Rep. 3rd row 3 times.
7th row: p.2, y.r.n., p.2 tog., rib to last 4 sts., p.4.
Work 1 more row.
Cast off in rib.

MAKING UP

Sew up raglan seams.
Sew up side and sleeve seams with small back-st., ensuring that ridges meet neatly.
Sew cast-on edge of button border neatly behind buttonhole border.
Sew on buttons.

Square-necked, T-shirt Sweater 1954

Stocking stitch sweater with all-in-one cap sleeves, square neck with rib border, and ribbed welts

★ Suitable for adventurous beginners

MATERIALS

Yarn
Wendy Ascot 4 ply
3(3:4:4:4) × 50g. balls

Needles
1 pair 3mm.
1 pair 3¼mm.
1 set of 5 double-pointed 3mm.
2 st. holders

MEASUREMENTS

Chest
61(66:71:76:82) cm.
24(26:28:30:32) in.
4/5(6/7:8/9:10/11:11/12) approx. age

Length
37(40:45:49:52) cm.
14½(15¾:17¾:19¼:20½) in.

TENSION

28 sts. and 36 rows = 10 cm. (4 in.) square over st. st. on 3¼mm. needles. If your tension square does not correspond to these measurements, adjust the needle size used.

ABBREVIATIONS

k. = knit; p. = purl; st(s). = stitch(es); inc. = increas(ing); dec. = decreas(ing); beg. = begin(ning); rem. = remain(ing); rep. = repeat; alt. = alternate; tog. = together; sl. = slip (transfer one stitch from left needle, knitwise unless otherwise stated, to right hand needle.); cont. = continue; patt. = pattern; foll. = following; folls. = follows; mm. = millimetres; cm. = centimetres; in. = inches; st. st. = stocking st.: one row k., one row p.; g. st. = garter st.: every row k.; incs. = increases; decs. = decreases; p.s.s.o. = pass the sl. st. over.

BACK

Cast on 82(90:98:106:114) sts. with 3mm. needles.
Work 8 cm. (3¼ in.) in k.1, p.1 rib, ending with a right side row.
Inc. row: p.2(2:3:3:4), * p. twice into next st., p.10(11:12:13:14), rep. from * 6 times, p. twice into next st., p. to end. [90(98:106:114:122) sts.]
Change to 3¼mm. needles.
Beg. with a k. row, work straight in st. st. until work measures 21(23:27:30:32) cm. (8¼(9:10½:11¾:12½) in.) from cast-on edge, ending with a p. row.

Shape Sleeves

Cast on 2 sts. at beg. of each of the next 10 rows. [110(118:126:134:142) sts.]
Cont. straight in st. st. until straight sleeve edge measures 11(12:13:14:15) cm. (4¼(4¾:5:5½:5¾) in.), ending with a p. row.

Shape Shoulders and Neck

Next row: cast off 7(8:9:10:11) sts., k. until there are 30(32:34:36:38) sts. on needle, turn, leaving rem. sts. on a spare needle.
Work 1 row straight.
** Cast off 6(7:8:9:10) sts. at beg. of next and foll. alt. row.
Work 1 row straight.
Cast off 6 sts. at beg. of next and foll. 2 alt. rows.
With right side facing sl. centre 36(38:40:42:44) sts. onto a holder.
Rejoin yarn to first of the rem. 37(40:43:46:49) sts.
Work 1 row straight.
Next row: cast off 7(8:9:10:11) sts. at beg. of next row.
Work 1 row straight.
Now work as for first side from ** to end.

FRONT

Work as for back until straight sleeve edge measures 8(9:10:11:12) cm. (3¼(3½: 4:4¼:4¾) in.), ending with a p. row. [110(118:126:134:142) sts.]

Shape Neck

Next row: k.37(40:43:46:49) sts., turn, leaving rem. sts. on a spare needle.
Cont. straight in st. st. until sleeve edge measures same as back sleeve, ending at side edge.

Shape Shoulder

Cast off 7(8:9:10:11) sts. at beg. of next row.
Work 1 row straight.
Cast off 6(7:8:9:10) sts. at beg. of next and foll. alt. row.
Work 1 row straight.
Cast off 6 sts. at beg. of next and foll. 2 alt. rows.
With right side facing, sl. centre 36(38:40: 42:44) sts. onto a holder.
Rejoin yarn to first of the rem. 37(40:43: 46:49) sts.
Work as for first side to end.

NECKBAND

Sew up shoulder seams.
With double-pointed needles, k. up sts. around neck edge as folls.:
1st round: 1st needle – k.36(38:40:42:44) sts. from holder at back neck edge; 2nd needle – k. up 36 sts. along neck edge of left shoulder; 3rd needle – k. across 36(38:40: 42:44) sts. at front neck edge; 4th needle – k. up 36 sts. along neck edge of right shoulder. [144(148:152:156:160) sts.]
Work in rounds of k.1, p.1 rib as folls.:
1st round: 1st needle – sl. 1, k.1, p.s.s.o., * k.1, p1, rep. from * to last 2 sts., k.2 tog.; work across rem. 3 needles in same way.
2nd round: work straight in rib as set on needles.
3rd round: 1st needle – sl.1, k.1, p.s.s.o., rib to last 2 sts., k.2 tog.; work across rem. 3 needles in same way.
Rep. 2nd and 3rd rounds 3 times.
Cast off loosely in rib.

SLEEVE BANDS

With 3mm. needles and right side facing, pick up and k.78(82:84:90:96) sts. along sleeve edge.
Work 9 rows in k.1, p.1 rib.
Cast off loosely in rib.

MAKING UP

Sew up side and sleeve seams.
Press.

Rabbit-design Sweater

1954

Long sweater in stocking stitch with contrasting, knitted-in rabbits on front, set-in sleeves and ribbed welts

★ Suitable for adventurous beginners

MATERIALS

Yarn
Emu Superwash 4 ply
3(4:4:4) × 50g. balls Main Col. A
1(1:1:1) × 50g. ball Col. B

Needles
1 pair 3mm.
1 pair 3¼mm.
2 st. holders

MEASUREMENTS

Chest
56(61:66:71) cm.
22(24:26:28) in.
2/3(4/5:6/7:8/9) approx. age

Length
34(36:38:41) cm.
13¼(14:15:16) in.

Sleeve Seam
25(29:32:35) cm.
9¾(11¼:12½:13¾) in.

TENSION

14 sts. and 18 rows = 5 cm. (2 in.) square over st. st. on 3¼mm. needles. If your tension square does not correspond to these measurements, adjust the needle size used.

ABBREVIATIONS

k.=knit; p:=purl; st(s).=stitch(es); inc.= increas(ing); dec.=decreas(ing); beg.= begin(ning); rem. = remain(ing); rep. = repeat; alt. = alternate; tog. = together; sl. = slip (transfer one stitch from left needle, knitwise unless otherwise stated, to right hand needle.); cont. = continue; patt. = pattern; foll. = following; folls. = follows; mm. = millimetres; cm. = centimetres; in. = inches; st. st. = stocking st.: one row k., one row p.; g. st. = garter st.: every row k.; incs. = increases; decs. = decreases; p.s.s.o. = pass slipped st. over.

BACK

Cast on 80(88:96:104) sts. with 3mm. needles and A.
Work 18 rows in k.1, p.1 rib.
Change to 3¼mm. needles.
Beg. with a k. row, work straight in st. st. until work measures 23(24:25:27) cm. (9(9½:9¾:10½) in.) from cast-on edge, ending with a p. row.

Shape Armholes

Cast off 3(4:5:6) sts. at beg. of next 2 rows and 2 sts. at beg. of foll. 2 rows.
5th row: k.1, sl.1, k.1, p.s.s.o., k. until 3 sts. rem., k.2 tog., k.1.
6th row: p.
Rep. 5th and 6th rows until 64(68:74:80) sts. rem.
Cont. straight until armholes measure 11(12:13:14) cm. (4¼(4¾:5:5½) in.), ending with a p. row.

Shape Shoulders

Cast off 8(9:10:11) sts. at beg. of next 2 rows and 9(9:10:11) sts. at beg. of foll. 2 rows.
Leave rem. 30(32:34:36) sts. on holder until required for neckband.

FRONT

Work as for back until 20 rows have been worked in st. st.
Now work the rabbit patt. from chart as folls.:
Odd-numbered k. rows, are read from right to left, and even-numbered p. rows, are read from left to right.
Carry yarn not in use loosely across back of work, catching it in every 5 sts. if necessary.
1st row: k.4(8:12:16) with A, join in B, and work 72 sts. from 1st row of chart, k.4(8:12:16) with A.
Work from 2nd to 15th row of chart, working the end 4(8:12:16) sts. on each row with A.
Break off B, and cont. entirely with A.
Beg. with a p. row, work as for back until armholes measure 6(7:8:9) cm. (2¼(2¾:

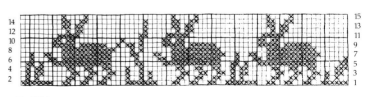

□ = Col A
▨ = Col B

3¼:3¾) in.), ending with a p. row.
[64(68:74:80) sts.]

Shape Neck
Next row: k.23(24:26:28), turn and work on these sts. leaving rem. sts. on a spare needle.
1st row: p.
2nd row: k. until 3 sts. rem., k.2 tog., k.1.
Rep. these 2 rows until 17(18:20:22) sts. rem.
** Cont. straight until armhole measures same as back armhole, ending at armhole edge.

Shape Shoulder
Cast off 8(9:10:11) sts. at beg. of next row, work 1 row straight then cast off rem. 9(9:10:11) sts.
With right side of work facing sl. next 18(20:22:24) sts. onto a holder until required for neckband, then rejoin A to first of rem. 23(24:26:28) sts.
1st row: k.
2nd row: p.
3rd row: k.1, sl.1, k.1, p.s.s.o., k. to end.
Rep. 2nd and 3rd rows until 17(18:20:22) sts. rem.
Now work from ** to end as for 1st shoulder.

SLEEVES
Cast on 44(46:48:50) sts. with 3mm. needles and A.
Work 18 rows in k.1, p.1 rib.
Change to 3¼mm. needles.
Beg. with a k. row, work 4 rows in st. st.
Next row: k.1, k. twice into next st., k. until 2 sts. rem., k. twice into next st., k.1.
Work 5 rows straight.
Rep. the last 6 rows until there are 62(66:70:74) sts.
Cont. straight until sleeve seam measures 25(29:32:35) cm. (9¾:11¼:12½:13¾) in.), ending with a p. row.

Shape Top
Cast off 3(4:5:6) sts. at beg. of next 2 rows and 2 sts. at beg. of foll. 2 rows.
5th row: k.1, sl.1, k.1, p.s.s.o., k. until 3 sts. rem., k.2 tog., k.1.
6th row: p.
Rep. 5th and 6th rows until 38 sts. rem.
Cast off 6 sts. at beg. of next 4 rows then cast off rem. 14 sts.

NECKBAND
Sew up right shoulder seam.
With right side of work facing, using A and 3mm. needles, pick up and k. 24 sts. down left front neck edge, k. across 18(20:22:24) sts. at centre front, pick up and k.24 sts. up right front neck edge and finally k. across 30(32:34:36) sts. at back neck edge. [96(100:104:108) sts.].
Work 6 rows in k.1, p.1 rib.
Cast off loosely in rib.

MAKING UP
Sew up remaining shoulder seam, carrying seams across neckband.
Set in sleeves.
Sew up side and sleeve seams.

Sleeveless Pullover in Cross-stitch 1937

Fine, sleeveless slipover in cross-stitch rib, with round neck and ribbed welts

★★ Suitable for knitters with some previous experience

MATERIALS

Yarn
Pingouin Pingolaine 4 ply
3(3:4:4) × 50g. balls

Needles
1 pair 2¾mm.
1 pair 3¼mm.

MEASUREMENTS

Chest
56(61:66:71) cm.
22(24:26:28) in.
2/3(4/5:6/7:8/9) approx. age

Length
33(37:39:43) cm.
13(14½:15¼:16¾) in.

TENSION

35 sts. and 38 rows = 10 cm. (4 in.) square over patt. on 3¼mm. needles. If your tension square does not correspond to these measurements, adjust the needle size used.

ABBREVIATIONS

k.=knit; p.=purl; st(s).=stitch(es); inc.= increas(ing); dec.=decreas(ing); beg.= begin(ning); rem. = remain(ing); rep. = repeat; alt. = alternate; tog. = together; sl. = slip (transfer one stitch from left needle, knitwise unless otherwise stated, to right hand needle.); cont. = continue;

patt. = pattern; foll. = following; folls. = follows; mm. = millimetres; cm. = centimetres; in. = inches; st. st. = stocking st.: one row k., one row p.; g. st. = garter st.: every row k.; incs. = increases; decs. = decreases; m.1 = make 1 st.: pick up horizontal loop lying before next st. and work into back of it; cross 3 = k. into front of 3rd st. on left needle, k. into front of 1st st., then k. into front of 2nd st., sl. all 3 sts. off needle tog.

BACK

** Cast on 87(95:101:109) sts. with 2¾mm needles.
Work in rib as folls.:
1st row (right side): k.1, * p.1, k.1, rep. from * to end.
2nd row: p.1, * k.1, p.1, rep. from * to end.
Rep. these 2 rows until work measures 5 cm. (2 in.), ending with a 1st row.
Next row: rib 2(6:5:9), * m.1, rib 4, rep. from * to last 1(5:4:8) sts., m.1, rib to end. [109(117:125:133) sts.]
Change to 3¼mm. needles and work in patt. as folls.:
1st row (right side): p.1, * k.3, p.1, rep. from * to end.
2nd row: k.1, * p.3, k.1, rep. from * to end.
3rd row: k.1, * p.1, k.3, rep. from * to end.
4th row: * p.3, k.1, rep. from * to last st., p.1.
5th row: k.1, * p.1, cross 3, rep. from * to end.
6th row: as 4th.
7th row: k.2, * p.1, k.3, rep. from * to last 3 sts., p.1, k.2.
8th row: p.2, * k.1, p.3, rep. from * to last 3 sts., k.1, p.2.
9th row: * k.3, p.1, rep. from * to last st., k.1.
10th row: p.1, * k.1, p.3, rep. from * to end.
11th row: * cross 3, p.1, rep. from * to last st., k.1.
12th row: p.1, * k.1, p.3, rep. from * to end.
These 12 rows form patt.
Cont. in patt. until back measures 20(22:23:26) cm. (7¾(8½:9:10¼) in.), ending with a wrong side row.

Shape Armholes
Keeping patt. straight, cast off 5 sts. at beg. of next 2 rows.
Dec. 1 st. at each end of next 7 rows.
Work 1 row.
Dec. 1 st. at each end of next and every alt. row until 77(83:91:97) sts. rem. **
Work straight in patt. until armholes

measure 13(15:16:17) cm. (5(5¾:6¼:6½) in.), ending with a right side row.

Shape Back Neck and Shoulders
Next row: patt. 27(28:30:31), cast off 23(27:31:35) sts. (including st. on needle after casting off), patt. 27(28:30:31).
Cont. on last 27(28:30:31) sts. for first side.
*** *Next row*: cast off 7(7:8:8), patt. to end.
Next row: cast off 3, patt. to end.
Rep. last 2 rows once more.
Cast off rem. 7(8:8:9) sts. ***
With right side facing, rejoin yarn to rem. sts., patt. to end.
Now work as given for first side from *** to ***.

FRONT

Work as for back from ** to **.
Work straight in patt. until armholes measure 8(10:10:11) cm. (3¼(4:4:4¼) in.), ending with a right side row.

Shape Neck
Next row: patt. 31(32:36:37), cast off 15(19:19:23) sts. (including st. on needle after casting off), patt. 31(32:36:37).
Cont. on last 31(32:36:37) sts. for first side.
**** Work 1 row.
Cast off 3 sts. at beg. of next and foll. alt. row.
Work 1 row.
Cast off 2 sts. at beg. of next and foll. 1(1:2:2) alt. rows.
Cont. straight on rem. 21(22:24:25) sts. until front matches back to beg. of shoulder shaping, ending at armhole edge.

Shape Shoulder
Cast off 7(7:8:8) sts. at beg. of next and foll. alt. row.
Work 1 row.
Cast off rem. 7(8:8:9) sts. ****.
With right side facing, rejoin yarn to rem. sts., patt. to end.
Work as for first side from **** to ****.

MAKING UP AND BORDERS

Sew up side and shoulder seams.

Neck border
Cast on 10 sts. with 2¾mm. needles and work in g. st. until border fits around neck, starting at left shoulder: sew in position as you work.
Cast off.
Sew border ends tog. at shoulder.

Armhole Borders
Work as for neck border.
Sew border ends tog. at underarm.

Twinset with Round or V Neckline

1957

Classic twinsets in stocking stitch with raglan sleeves, sweater with long or short sleeves, cardigan with high or V-neck buttoning

★ Suitable for beginners

NB twinset cardigan was photographed without buttons

MATERIALS

Yarn
Rowan botany wool 3 ply
Long Sleeved Sweater:
6(6:8:8:9:10) × 25g. hanks
Short Sleeved Sweater:
5(5:6:7:8:9) × 25g. hanks
Cardigan:
6(6:8:8:9:10) × 25g. hanks

Needles
1 pair 2¼mm.
1 pair 3mm.
1 set of 4 double-pointed 2¼mm. for sweater
safety pin
st. holders

Buttons
7 for round-neck cardigan
or
6 for v-neck cardigan

MEASUREMENTS

Chest
61(66:71:76:82:87) cm.
24(26:28:30:32:34) in.
4/5(6/7:8/9:10/11:12/13:14/15) approx. age

Length
Sweater:
37(40:44:46:51:54) cm.
14½(15¾:17¼:18:20:21¼) in.
Cardigan:
39(43:46:48:53:57) cm.
15¼(16¾:18:18¾:20¾:22¼) in.

Sleeve Seam
Short-sleeved sweater:
8(9:10:11:12:13) cm.
3¼(3½:4:4¼:4¾:5) in.
Long-sleeved sweater:
23(27:31:36:41:42) cm.
9(10½:12¼:14:16:16½) in.
Cardigan Sleeve Seam:
24(28:32:37:42:43) cm.
9½(11:12½:14½:16½:16¾) in.

TENSION

32 sts. and 40 rows = 10 cm. (4 in.) square over st. st. on 3mm. needles. If your tension square does not correspond to these measurements, adjust the needle size used.

ABBREVIATIONS

k. = knit; p. = purl; st(s). = stitch(es); inc. = increas(ing); dec. = decreas(ing); beg. = begin(ning); rem. = remain(ing); rep. = repeat; alt. = alternate; tog. = together; sl. = slip (transfer one stitch from left needle, knitwise unless otherwise stated, to right hand needle.); cont. = continue; patt. = pattern; foll. = following; folls. = follows; mm. = millimetres; cm. = centimetres; in. = inches; st. st. = stocking st.: one row k., one row p.; g. st. = garter st.: every row k.; incs. = increases; decs. = decreases; p.s.s.o. = pass the sl. st. over.

SWEATER BACK

Cast on 104(112:120:128:136:144) sts. with 2¼mm. needles.
Work 6 cm. (2¼ in.) in k.1, p.1 rib.
Change to 3mm. needles and st. st.
Cont. straight until work measures 23(25:28:29:33:35) cm. (9(9¾:11:11¼:13:13¾) in.), ending with a p. row.

Shape Raglans
Cast off 4(5:6:7:8:9) sts. at beg. of next 2 rows.
Dec. 1 st. at each end of next 7 rows.
Next row: p.
11th row: k.2, k.2 tog., k. to last 4 sts., sl.1, k.1, p.s.s.o., k.2.
12th row: p.
Rep. last 2 rows until 36(38:40:42:44:46)

sts. rem., ending with a p. row.
Leave sts. on holder.

SWEATER FRONT

Work as for back until 56(58:60:62:64:66) sts. rem., ending with a k. row.

Shape Neck
Next row: p.22, turn.
Finish this side first.
** Cont. dec. 1 st. at raglan edge on every alt. row, AT THE SAME TIME dec. 1 st. at neck edge on next 5 rows, then on every alt. row 3 times, then on every 3rd row until 3 sts. rem.
Next row: p.3.
Next row: k.1, k.2 tog.
Next row: p.2.
Cast off.
Sl. centre 12(14:16:18:20:22) sts. onto st. holder for neck.
Rejoin yarn to rem. sts. and p. to end.
Work to match first side from ** to end.

SWEATER SHORT SLEEVES

Cast on 66(70:74:78:82:86) sts. with 2¼mm. needles.
Work 3 cm. (1¼ in.) in k.1, p.1 rib.
Change to 3mm. needles and st. st.
Inc. 1 st. at each end of next and every 4th row until there are 78(84:90:96:102:108) sts.
Work 1 row.

Shape Raglan
Cast off 4(5:6:7:8:9) sts. at beg. of next 2 rows.
3rd row: k.2, k.2 tog., k. to last 4 sts., sl.1, k.1, p.s.s.o., k.2.
4th row: p.
Rep. last 2 rows until 16 sts. rem.
Leave sts. on holder.

SWEATER LONG SLEEVES

Cast on 48(50:54:56:58:60) sts. with 2¼mm. needles.
Work 5 cm. (2 in.) in k.1, p.1 rib.
Change to 3mm. needles and st. st.
Inc. 1 st. at each end of next and every foll. 4th(5th:5th:5th:6th:6th) row until there are 78(84:90:96:102:108) sts.
Cont. straight until sleeve measures 23(27:31:36:41:42) cm. (9(10½:12¼:14:16:16½) in.), ending with a p. row.

Shape Raglan
Cast off 4(5:6:7:8:9) sts. at beg. of next 2 rows.
3rd row: k.2, k.2 tog., k. to last 4 sts., sl.1, k.1, p.s.s.o., k.2.
4th row: p.
Rep. last 2 rows until 16 sts. rem.
Leave sts. on holder.

SWEATER NECKBAND

Sew up raglan seams.
With right side facing and set of 2¼mm. needles, pick up and k.36(38:40:42:44:46) sts. from holder at back, 16 sts. from left sleeve, 20 sts. down left front, 12(14:16:18:20:22) sts. from holder at front, 20 sts. up right front and 16 sts. from right sleeve. [120(124:128:132:136:140) sts.]

Work 5 cm. (2 in.) in k.1, p.1 rib.
Cast off loosely in rib.

SWEATER MAKING UP

Press work lightly with warm iron over damp cloth.
Sew up side and sleeve seams.
Press seams.
Turn neckband in half onto wrong side and sl. st. loosely down.

ROUND-NECK CARDIGAN BACK

Cast on 108(116:124:132:140:148) sts. with 2¼mm. needles.
Work 8 cm. (3¼ in.) in k.1, p.1 rib.
Change to 3mm. needles and st. st.
Cont. straight until work measures 24(27:29:30:34:37) cm. (9½(10½:11¼:11¾:13¼:14½) in.), ending with a p. row.

Shape Raglans
Cast off 5(6:7:8:9:10) sts. at beg. of next 2 rows.
Now dec. 1 st. at each end of next 7 rows.
Next row: p.
11th row: k.2, k.2 tog., k. to last 4 sts., sl.1, k.1, p.s.s.o., k.2.
12th row: p.
Rep. last 2 rows until 36(38:40:42:44:46) sts. rem., ending with a p. row.
Leave sts. on holder.

ROUND-NECK CARDIGAN LEFT FRONT

Cast on 51(55:59:63:67:71) sts. with 2¼mm. needles.
Work 8 cm. (3¼ in.) in k.1, p.1 rib, beg. alt. rows p.1.
Change to 3mm. needles and st. st.
Work until front measures same as back to armholes, ending with a p. row (end with a k. row on right front). **

Shape Raglan
Cast off 5(6:7:8:9:10) sts. at beg. of next row.
P. 1 row (omit this row on right front).
Dec. 1 st. at armhole edge on next 7 rows.
P. 1 row.
11th row: k.2, k.2 tog., k. to end.
12th row: p.
Rep. last 2 rows until 26(27:28:29:30:31) sts. rem., ending with a p. row.

Shape Neck
1st row: k.2, k.2 tog., k.19, turn, sl. rem. 3(4:5:6:7:8) sts. onto holder.
Still dec. at armhole edge as before, dec. 1 st. at neck edge on next 4 rows then at neck edge on every alt. row 3 times, then every 3rd row until 3 sts. rem., ending with a p. row.
Next row: k.1, k.2 tog.
Next row: p.2.
Cast off.

ROUND-NECK CARDIGAN RIGHT FRONT

Work as for left front, reversing all shapings.
Work raglan shaping as folls.:
Work to last 4 sts., sl.1, k.1, p.s.s.o., k.2.

ROUND-NECK CARDIGAN SLEEVES

Cast on 52(54:56:58:60:62) sts. with 2¼mm. needles.
Work 5 cm. (2 in.) in k.1, p.1 rib.
Change to 3mm. needles and st. st.
Inc. 1 st. at each end of next and every foll. 5th(5th:5th:5th:6th:6th) row until there are 82(88:94:100:106:112) sts.
Work until sleeve measures 24(28:32:37:42:43) cm. (9½(11:12½:14½:16½:16¾) in.), ending with a p. row.

Shape Raglan
Cast off 5(6:7:8:9:10) sts. at beg. of next 2 rows.
3rd row: k.2, k.2 tog., k. to last 4 sts., sl.1, k.1, p.s.s.o., k.2.
4th row: p.
Rep. last 2 rows until 16 sts. rem.
Leave sts. on holder.

ROUND-NECK CARDIGAN BUTTON BAND

Cast on 12 sts. with 2¼mm. needles.
Work in k.1, p.1 rib until band is long enough, when slightly stretched, to fit up front to beg. of neck.
Sl. sts. onto a safety pin.
Break off yarn.
Sew in place.
Mark positions for 7 buttons, placing 1st hole 1 cm. (½ in.) from lower edge and allowing for last one to be in the centre of 2 cm. (¾ in.) neckband which is worked later.

ROUND-NECK CARDIGAN BUTTONHOLE BAND

Work as for button band, working buttonholes to correspond with positions marked for buttons as folls.:
1st buttonhole row: rib 4, cast off 4, rib to end.
Next row: rib to cast-off sts., cast on 4, rib to end.

ROUND-NECK CARDIGAN NECKBAND

Sew up raglan seams.
With right side of work facing and 2¼mm. needles, rib 15(16:17:18:19:20) sts. from holders at right front (including 12 sts. from front band), pick up and k.16 sts. from right front, 16 sts. from right sleeve, 36(38:40:42:44:46) sts. from holder at back, 16 sts. from left sleeve, 16 sts. down left front and rib 15(16:17:18:19:20) sts. from holders at left front (including 12 sts. from front band). [130(134:138:142:146:150) sts.]
Work 5 rows in k.1, p.1 rib.
Work buttonhole on next 2 rows.
Rib 10 rows.
Work buttonhole on next 2 rows.
Rib 5 rows.
Cast off loosely in rib.

ROUND-NECK CARDIGAN MAKING UP

Sew up side and sleeve seams.
Fold neckband in half onto wrong side

and sew in place.
Neaten double buttonhole on neckband.
Sew on buttons.
Press seams.

V-NECK CARDIGAN BACK AND SLEEVES

Work as for round-necked cardigan, but cast off rem. sts.

V-NECK CARDIGAN LEFT FRONT

Work as for round-necked cardigan to **.

Shape Raglan and Neck
1st row: cast off 5(6:7:8:9:10) sts., k. to last 2 sts., k.2 tog.
2nd row: work to end.
3rd row: k.2 tog., work to end.
4th row: work to last 2 sts., p.2 tog.
5th row: k.2 tog., work to last 2 sts., k.2 tog.
6th row: as 4th.
7th row: as 3rd.
8th row: as 4th.
9th row: k.2, k.2 tog., k. to last 2 sts., k.2 tog.
10th row: work to end.
11th row: k.2, k.2 tog., work to end.
12th row: as 10th.
Rep. 9th to 12th rows until 6 sts. rem., ending with a 10th row.
Dec. at raglan edge only until 2 sts. rem., ending with a p. row.
Cast off.

V-NECK CARDIGAN RIGHT FRONT

Work as for left front, reversing all shapings.
Work raglan shaping as folls.:
Work to last 4 sts., sl.1, k.1, p.s.s.o., k.2.

V-NECK CARDIGAN FRONT BAND

Sew up raglan seams.
Sew up side and sleeve seams.
Cast on 12 sts. with 2¼mm. needles and work in k.1, p.1 rib until band is long enough, when slightly stretched, to fit up left front, across back neck and down front to first front dec., sewing in place as you k.
1st buttonhole row: rib 4, cast off 4, rib to end.
Next row: rib to cast off sts., cast on 4 sts., rib to end.
Mark position for buttons on button band, first to match with buttonhole already worked, the last to come 1 cm. (½ in.) from lower edge, rem. 4 equally spaced between.
Cont. in rib, working buttonholes as before to match with positions marked for buttons.
Cast off in rib.

V-NECK CARDIGAN MAKING UP

Sew on buttons.
Press seams.